TAKE CARE
of
YOUR TYPE

AN ENNEAGRAM GUIDE TO SELF-CARE

CHRISTINA S. WILCOX

TILLER PRESS

New York   London   Toronto   Sydney   New Delhi

An Imprint of Simon & Schuster, Inc.
1230 Avenue of the Americas
New York, NY 10020

First Tiller Press hardcover edition December 2020

TILLER PRESS and colophon are trademarks of Simon & Schuster, Inc.

For information about special discounts for bulk purchases, please contact Simon & Schuster Special Sales at 1-866-506-1949 or business@simonandschuster.com.

The Simon & Schuster Speakers Bureau can bring authors to your live event. For more information or to book an event, contact the Simon & Schuster Speakers Bureau at 1-866-248-3049 or visit our website at www.simonspeakers.com.

Interior design by Jennifer Chung

Manufactured in the United States of America

1   3   5   7   9   10   8   6   4   2

Library of Congress Cataloging-in-Publication Data
Names: Wilcox, Christina S, author.
Title: Take care of your type : an enneagram guide to self-care / Christina S. Wilcox.
Description: New York : Tiller Press, [2020] | Identifiers: LCCN 2020026537 (print) |
LCCN 2020026538 (ebook) | ISBN 9781982157944 (hardcover) |
ISBN 9781982157968 (ebook) | Subjects: LCSH: Enneagram. | Classification: LCC
BF698.35.E54 W54 2020 (print) | LCC BF698.35.E54 (ebook) | DDC 155.2/6—dc23
LC record available at https://lccn.loc.gov/2020026537
LC ebook record available at https://lccn.loc.gov/2020026538

ISBN 978-1-9821-5794-4
ISBN 978-1-9821-5796-8 (ebook)

☾

FOR THOSE LONGING TO GROW AND
SHOW COMPASSION TOWARD THEMSELVES

CONTENTS

INTRODUCTION

Hello, my friends and friends I haven't met yet! First off, I want to thank you for picking up this book. I wrote it with high hopes and big prayers that it would change the way you view your self-worth, and that it would also give you practical advice and tools for taking care of who you are given your personality.

All of the self-care advice in this book is based on the nine types of the Enneagram personality system. In case you're unfamiliar with the Enneagram, though I can't imagine it's brand-new to you if you're reading this book, here is a brief overview of what it entails and how it can be used to inform better self-care practices for your specific personality type.

Over the past few years, the Enneagram has taken the internet by storm. People want to understand themselves on a deeper level, so they go online, take a quick Enneagram assessment, discover their type, and then dive into the endless amounts of information and creative memes related to it. Although there is nothing wrong with doing this, many people don't know that the Enneagram is actually a sacred, centuries-old system. Some say it was invented in the year 1915, but it is also theorized to have been developed by monks centuries earlier. The Enneagram was originally used for intense, purposeful self-reflection and was taught under the guidance of a mentor with the intention of healing a person's emotional wounds from as far back as childhood. As it has become westernized, it has lost a lot of its original depth, and though the intention of this book is not to provide an exhaustive history and education of the Enneagram, I did want to touch on that briefly so you can better understand how I view the concept of self-care through its lens.

Before you can really begin using and benefiting from this book, you will need to know these three things:

1. THERE ARE NINE ENNEAGRAM TYPES:

TYPE 1: The Idealist
TYPE 2: The Helper
TYPE 3: The Achiever
TYPE 4: The Individualist
TYPE 5: The Observer
TYPE 6: The Loyalist
TYPE 7: The Enthusiast
TYPE 8: The Challenger
TYPE 9: The Peacemaker

2. EACH INDIVIDUAL HAS A LITTLE BIT OF EVERY ENNEAGRAM TYPE WITHIN THEM, BUT THE TYPE THAT IS DOMINANT OVER THE REST IS CONSIDERED YOUR TYPE.

What determines your Enneagram type are the core desires, fears, and motivations that bring up the most emotion for you as you read them.

Through reading the chapters of this book, which are each prefaced with a particular type's core traits, you will become intimately acquainted with all nine Enneagram types and discover which one is yours.

3. YOUR ENNEAGRAM TYPE CAN HAVE WHAT IS CALLED A "WING."

Imagine a bird: it has two wings that it uses—one on its left, the other on its right. Either the left or right can be stronger or used more frequently than the other, and we would call that the dominant wing of the bird. The same is true of Enneagram types. Once you determine your type, you may discover you have a dominant "wing" as well. Whatever wing you have will *only* be directly to the left or directly to the right of your core type, numerically. Here are all the potential wing combinations in the Enneagram:

1W2, 1W9

2W1, 2W3

3W2, 3W4

4W3, 4W5

5W4, 5W6

6W5, 6W7

7W6, 7W8

8W7, 8W9

9W8, 9W1

If you are a 2W1, for example, your core type is Type 2, or The Helper. But you may find yourself heavily relating to the qualities and behavioral patterns of a Type 1, or Idealist, as well, which would give you a "1" wing.

Although you may already know your Enneagram type and want to flip directly to that chapter, I encourage you to read this book from the beginning—because at the end of every chapter, I list several important ways you can love and support someone with that specific Enneagram type on their self-care journey. Doing this may allow you to better understand the people you have had, will have, and currently have in your life. So please read through every chapter, take notes, and learn as much as you can about the personalities that surround you in life. Discovering another person's Enneagram type can be just as insightful and life-changing as discovering your own.

Now I want to define the kind of "self-care" I discuss in this book because it may be different from what you're envisioning. The type of self-care that I have chosen to focus on in these pages does not only revolve around practical, fun ways to stay healthy and take care of your physical self. Yes, I believe in the power of a relaxing bath, rejuvenating face mask, or brisk walk, and I have experienced the power of what a long hot shower, a delicious homemade dessert, and a great conversation with a friend can do for the soul. But as I have further immersed myself in my journey of self-discovery, I have found that self-care involves so much more than just looking after your physical body. In fact, the pursuit of physical self-care alone is rather shallow, in my opinion. Because no matter how hard you work to change and refresh what's only visible on the outside, your inner struggles will still be there.

Oftentimes, we expect these physical-driven self-care practices to transform something within us. There is absolutely nothing wrong with "glowing up," losing weight, or focusing on taking care of your body in a healthy way, but that on its own won't bring you happiness and peace of mind. It's important to understand that self-care is not just about looking good; it's about feeling whole. It's about healing the things that haunt us at night, so that we can not only go on to be our best selves but also be equipped with the tools to help us effectively deal with hurt or harm as we encounter it in the future.

That being said, even the kind of self-care I explore in this book can't always provide the true confidence, sustainable happiness, and internal change many of us desire. I am not a mental health expert or counselor; I'm simply a young woman who truly believes in the power of this system and who long wished I had someone to guide me through understanding my emotions and behavioral patterns. And I hope to be that someone for you. If you find yourself dealing with PTSD, anxiety, depression, OCD, or other mental illnesses, know that you're not alone and I'm right there fighting alongside you. But I do ask upfront that you do not set the expectation that this book will completely heal you, because it won't. Healing takes time. It takes work. It can take therapy and medication and spiritual awakening. All of the self-care tips I provide in this book revolve around cultivating deep, inner reflection for the purpose of self-growth, and I wholeheartedly hope this reflection sets you on the path to healing and treating yourself better every day. However, I alone cannot heal you, and neither can these pages, so I encourage you to seek all the help you need.

Ultimately, I want you to know I wrote this book so that I could shed light on deep and authentic self-care for all of the Enneagram types. We can take care of our physical body as much as we want, but if we ignore the practice of tending to our soul, heart, and mind as well, we will never grow from our negative perceptions and treatment of both ourselves and others. So I hope you will join me on this new journey of tending to your whole, beautiful, deserving self every day and night. Let's take care of your type.

THE IDEALIST

ETHICAL, BALANCED,
NOBLE, DISCERNING, FOCUSED

CORE DESIRES:

To be "good," balanced, and honorable

CORE FEARS:

Being "bad" or imperfect

ULTIMATE MOTIVATIONS:

To successfully meet the high standards
they set for themselves, to be impervious
to criticism, to bring correctness
and truth to the world, to live out their
"sense of mission," to be right

AFFIRMATION:

"I am good."

Enneagram Type 1s are people who can walk into a room and quickly see what needs to be improved. They are the friends you always go to for advice or who hold you accountable for your goals and actions, and they are usually extremely hard on themselves when they make mistakes. They are naturally inclined to live a life of order, however they define or see that order. Living their life to the fullest means striving toward the ideals and high expectations they have set for themselves. I refer to Type 1s as "Idealists," but Idealists are usually known in the Enneagram practice as "Perfectionists" or "Reformers" because, at the end of the day, they are always pursuing what they believe to be "better" or noble. While this may indeed be perfection, each Type 1 has a different idea of what that looks like. And ultimately, I think, more than perfection Idealists crave the ideal situation, the ideal persona, the most controlled, efficient, and balanced version of themselves and others. Because of this, they will avoid making mistakes at all costs, and they usually keep their physical and emotional appetites in check.

You Might Be an Idealist If . . .

- You feel like you have an inner critic who is continually questioning the morality and efficiency of every choice or move you make.
- You constantly notice what's wrong in a room or in a situation, and you cannot rest until it's fixed.
- No matter how great a job you did on a project or at work, you can still find something you wish you had done better.

- You have some bottled-up anger within you that feels more like resentment. When you finally reach your tipping point, you direct your frustration intensely toward yourself or others.
- You strive to be an optimistic yet realistic person. You want to be balanced in everything that you feel.
- Whenever you're upset or feel burdened by a cause you're fighting for, you find yourself tapping into a lot of creativity, while also running the risk of burnout.
- Although you may not admit it, you enjoy the finer things in life.
- People assume you don't like to go on adventures and have fun, but you actually enjoy throwing caution to the wind and trying something new every once in a while.
- You are constantly showing up for and loving on your closest friends.
- You are fiercely independent.
- You feel most passionate about righting injustices, even if that means you have to make sacrifices in order to end them.

1W2

Leaning into their 2 wing, these Idealists are more focused on empathy and community. Rather than perfecting society as a whole, they are focused on making the lives of individuals and their loved ones nothing short of heavenly. The "good" that they desire to do is usually focused toward others as well, and they put a lot of pressure on themselves to show up as a shining role model for the community in which they are invested. They want to be the perfect child, spouse, friend, coworker, etc., and can sometimes get lost in their desire to be above reproach in their relationships. A little more outgoing and playful than 1W9s, these 1s are advice-giving, wise, and emotionally expressive. If you have a 1W2 in your life, consider yourself lucky.

1W9

These Idealists usually are more reserved and self-composed, but are emotionally generous when you crack open their shell. 1W9s are visionaries, and are often thinking about what is right for the world as a whole. They are more prone than a 1W2 to optimistic thinking, and strive for an order that is just as harmonious as it is organized. Their systems must not only be perfect but also bring the most peace to their life. These Idealists can forget to speak up in moments of pressure because they do not want to be seen as disrespectful, angry, or demanding, which are all things they view as being "wrong." Vulnerability is difficult for them as well, because they fear being cut off from their relationships if they show their imperfections. They are more likely to stay in on a Friday night in the name of coziness and relaxation. And the depths to which 1W9s care about justice and the good of everyone is deeply admirable. They make the world a better place.

WHY IDEALISTS NEED SELF-CARE

Enneagram Type 1s seek what is right and just above all else, sometimes at the cost of open-mindedness and authenticity. They ultimately desire for their world to be perfect, and this desire can sometimes keep them from missing out on the beauty and wonder that surrounds them, even if it's a little messy. They can end up living regulated, lonely, and all-around unhealthy lives, physically and mentally, if they do not take care of themselves. Type 1s, you need self-care so that you can actually achieve justice and order, while also experiencing life fully without reservation or guilt. Through the practice of self-care and reflection, Idealists will discover that they are not defined by their mistakes. In fact, they will become more accepting of themselves, their flaws, and the imperfections of their world, and grow to be wonder-filled individuals.

SELF-CARE PRACTICES FOR TYPE 1S

Let Yourself Struggle

Idealists are continually striving to overcome their imperfections. Whatever they deem most valuable to them in life, they are determined to do it with the most excellence. They want their work, their heart, their actions to be above reproach. They want others to see them as good examples. Idealists don't like to be seen as anything less than perfect, making it difficult for them to process failure or anything that does not live up to their high standards. Admitting they struggle or feeling like they aren't meeting their standards crushes them to an extent that most people don't realize. When Idealists strive for what is ideal, they give everything in order to achieve the perfect scenario. And when the grade does not come back as they had hoped, when they did not get the raise they believe they deserved, when that one thing didn't get checked off their to-do list, it takes a big hit to Idealists' well-being. But in these moments of "failure," a growing Idealist can find self-compassion. I want Idealists to know that even when a grade, or a certain piece of feedback, isn't what you thought it would be, accepting that you will struggle in life no matter how much work you put into it will reconnect you to your humanity. And your humanity is not disgusting or wrong; it's beautiful. It's learning, blooming, and becoming—with each trial and triumph. The improvement you're seeking can often be found in the midst of the struggle, so learn to sit with it. Know that you're loved in it.

Take Intentional Time to Be Alone

I think it's good for every Enneagram type to take intentional time to be alone every now and then, but I think it's especially important for Idealists. Idealists spend so much of their time making sure everything is in proper order, or checking in on others to ensure they're on top of what they need to do, that they often forget to take time for themselves, regardless of whether they're an introvert or an extrovert. Idealists believe that the fate of the world depends on them somehow. They are highly dutiful and have a hard time taking time for themselves to recuperate from this immense pressure. Many Idealists I know say that the most beneficial thing they have ever done for themselves in regard to freeing themselves from the pressure to manage everything in their lives is taking a trip on their own—exploring a new place, letting their adventurous side loose, or allowing themselves to take time to self-reflect and just to enjoy life! So, Idealists, I encourage you to plan some time to just be alone and free—someplace away from where all of your perceived responsibilities or pressures are located.

Bring On the Nostalgia

Idealists have a love for all things classic. Many Type 1s I know love Old Hollywood stars, adore vintage finds, and enjoy reminiscing about pleasant past memories, and a way Idealists can take care of themselves more frequently is to lean into this love more often. Go through old scrapbooks and journals, reflect on how far you've come, and take note of how much you've actually grown. See all of the ways you've improved, all of the incredible changes and good efforts you have made; you are not a failure! Nostalgia can be good for Idealists because of how much it enables them to see how hard they've worked and how much they've accomplished over the years. So turn on your favorite classic movie, bake your favorite recipe, invite over your oldest friend, and spend time reminiscing. Process the present, and hope for the future, by first appreciating all of the things that made you who are in this moment— how you've learned, what things have become a part of your every day, the big things and little things. Enjoy the nostalgia!

Jump into Something Impractical

Although Idealists are, well, idealistic, they can also be relatively practical individuals. They despise inefficiency or laziness of any kind, which can make it difficult for them to let their hair down and relax their shoulders. It's hard for Idealists to pursue passion projects, or creative endeavors, if they don't have a step-by-step plan and an assurance of excellence through the process. They are internally always at war with themselves because they have vivid expectations and dreams for themselves, but can become paralyzed by this constant internal evaluating and correcting. A close Idealist friend of mine once told me that one of the best self-care rituals she decided to introduce into her life was the pursuit of *im*practicality. Meaning, taking time to do things that don't necessarily make her life better, or scheduling days off or blocks of time that allow her to take breaks from cleaning, organizing, working, planning, or anything she feels pressured to do. Sometimes she'll spend her pursuit of impracticality turning the music up in her room so she can have a dance party by herself. Other times she'll listen to music and simply lie on her bed and stare at the ceiling. She's very passionate about cooking and trying new recipes, so sometimes she'll use her day off as a baking day. The pursuit of pleasure and impracticality on those days has changed her life and brought her so much joy—not to mention helped her rest up for the coming week. So, my dear Idealist, jump into something impractical. Schedule it. Pursue it. You deserve the break.

Let Go of Control

If you've ever met an Idealist, you would probably stereotype them as fairly controlling individuals. Some Idealists want everything to be a certain way, down to how dishes are stacked in the kitchen cabinets, while other Idealists are more focused on perfecting other areas of their life. They usually have a particular way they want to eat, live, and work, and they're unafraid of making that known to others. I know an Idealist who pursues perfection in taking care of the outdoor landscaping at his house. He is determined to create the most pleasurable, perfect backyard experience for anyone who spends time there, and he cannot rest until the job is done. He'll always find something new to fix, even where there may not be something to fix, because the thought of not having his hands on something makes him physically and emotionally uncomfortable. As an Idealist, whatever you seek to have control over the most—maybe it's aesthetics, maybe it's school, maybe it's your appearance, maybe it's your job—one of the best things you can do for your mental health is to let go of that control sometimes. You're allowed to fight the urge to make everything perfect. Let others do things the way they think is right. Let your partner plant the flowers they like in your garden, even if they're not what you want. While other people should of course respect your space, you should also try to respect the opinions and ideas of others even if they don't match up perfectly with yours. Others having different opinions or preferences than yours doesn't necessarily make them wrong, it makes them different. Drop control out of your hands and take up acceptance instead—of yourself, of others, and of where you are right now in life.

Throw a Party for No Reason

Idealists love to celebrate, but they can be prone to feeling guilty for loving celebration because it often involves indulgence and rest. If you're a Type 1, a wonderful self-care practice would be to start incorporating more celebration into your life, but not necessarily for a particular reason. Show yourself that you're worthy of celebration even on days when nothing got done because, maybe, doing nothing is exactly what you needed. Being in tune with yourself is a reason to celebrate! Idealists are happiest when they're celebrating life, not just for what they're accomplishing or for how they're growing but simply because they're alive. So throw a party for no reason. Treat yourself to your favorite dessert even when you don't feel like you've "earned" it. Celebration is not something that always needs to be earned; it needs to be nurtured. If you feel as though you *need* to have a reason to celebrate, then try making it simple: *I woke up today. I got to see my best friend. My favorite artist just released a new album. The weather was beautiful today. My tea was just the way I like it.* Keep an eye out for not just what needs to be fixed but what is also a cause for joy and celebration!

Prioritize Community

I believe that a lot of Idealists naturally prioritize their community of friends and loved ones because it's the right thing to do in their eyes, but I want to challenge Idealists to deepen their prioritization in a way that, while maybe uncomfortable at first, is necessary for their mental health. Idealists have this idea that they have to bear everything alone. Talking to someone else about their struggles can be viewed as "wrong" in their mind, and they would rather not open up about their mistakes or past traumas on the chance that they could be condemned or criticized. The truth is, though, discussing your pain with those you love and trust and confiding in them about the voice of your inner critic will only help you grow and heal any past pain. It will help you learn to laugh at yourself a little bit more, and help you give yourself grace. I'm challenging you to really prioritize community so that you can let yourself be cared for deeply by them, to be accepted for your secret goofiness, to be seen for your true self, not just your controlled self.

Forgive Yourself

Idealists, an incomplete checklist does not make you a failure. A past mistake does not define your goodness. Emotions don't make you corruptible or evil. Declining grades, a forgotten commitment, a moment of weakness does not define your identity unless you let it. As you now know, Idealists have a LOUD, badgering inner critic that lives inside of them, constantly picking out every flaw in their processes, in their efficiency, in their humanness. Some of the best self-care Idealists can do is fight their inner critic by becoming their own inner encourager. Yes, this takes work. It takes energy. It takes working against your natural tendencies. But you deserve to be encouraged, and not just by others but by yourself. You're allowed to be proud of yourself. You're allowed to know your worth is not dependent on your goodness. Your value is not measured by the ruler you keep close to your waist, your standards, or your work ethic. And as you become your own hype man, you will begin to find the rhythm of continual self-compassion and forgiveness. Did you know that as an Idealist, the hardest person for you to forgive is yourself? But if someone else is worth forgiving, then you are worth forgiving. There is no checklist for self-forgiveness because you are intrinsically loved no matter what you do or how you behave. So forgive yourself. Encourage yourself. You deserve it.

Find a Creative Outlet

Like many of us, Idealists when stressed or upset can be moody and melancholic. But they also may find this is when they feel most inspired. When they feel the most broken or upset, most Idealists I've interacted with find themselves wanting to put that sadness or grief or heartache or confusion into something other than work. Self-expression through art, music, food, dance, and theater is something many Idealists have deep appreciation for, but are often too apprehensive to participate in themselves. Rather than being afraid of this blossoming creativity, Idealists can learn to lean into it by finding a few different creative hobbies to try during moments of stress or intense emotion that can feel all-encompassing. Creativity will not only help you process these moments in a healthier way but it will also help free your mind from the need to be perfect. Self-care for Idealists is often about allowing themselves to practice more self-expression, because it helps them learn what being vulnerable with themselves can look like. It promotes emotional honesty as well as just giving an Idealist another way to process that still feels productive!

Gain Perspective

Idealists are highly observant and can notice when the placement of an object or the vibe of a room is even slightly off. They walk into a room and can't help but automatically notice what needs to be corrected, which only fuels their struggle with perfectionism. All of the Idealists I've spoken to say it's hard for them to see the big picture in their pursuits because they get so focused on one particular step or one small part of what they're doing. They believe that once every single piece of the puzzle is excellent, then they themselves will finally be excellent. Where this habit really becomes problematic is when Idealists become so focused on perfecting that one step or "puzzle piece" that they forget about the full picture. It's important for Idealists to take the time to gain perspective when they become hyperfocused on one particular task. Some practical ways you as an Idealist can encourage yourself to practice this new behavior is by adding phrases like "breathe," "slow down," or "take a second" to sticky notes or pieces of paper you can hang up in places you look at often, or by setting alarms on your phone with similar sayings. You can also practice opening up to your trusted friends about your plans so that they can be there for you in moments of refocusing and reprioritizing.

It's Okay to Be Angry

Idealists don't ever want to think of themselves as angry people. They tend to keep a tight rein on their temper, and if they do let you know how they feel, it's usually through the expression of criticism and frustration, not all-out anger. This is because Idealists believe that the emotion of anger itself is harmful. As with the rest of their emotional impulses, Idealists attempt to control and stifle their anger, but what they need to be aware of is that sometimes their suppression of anger can lead to others feeling as though they are walking on eggshells around them. They may still sense when an Idealist is angry, but because Idealists don't openly show it, others may start to worry that they're making the wrong moves around them. What many Idealists don't realize is that when they suppress their anger over and over again they are actually building deep, inner resentment toward others and toward themselves. This can lead to bitterness and emotional breakage within Idealists, to the point where it can be damaging for those with whom they are in relationships as well. So although this may go against the nature of the Idealist, a way they can practice better self-care is by being okay with being angry. Let yourself fully feel your anger, and then calmly and respectfully, to the best of your ability, confide in your partner or friend about it—not approaching the conversation with criticism of whatever the other person did to have made you upset, but engaging in the conversation by discussing how that action made you feel.

Take Yourself Out of the Running

One of the most beautiful things I've heard a healthy, self-aware Idealist say is that they've taken themselves "out of the running." In an Idealist's mind, they're continually competing against themselves. Every standard they have gets raised slightly higher when they come closer to reaching it. They do this because they want to see how close to perfect they can get. As you know, Idealists generally want to be above reproach. Any misstep they make, any thing they overlooked that could have potentially been made better, eats them up inside. I once heard a Type 1 on a podcast say, "Thinking that I did a good job at work that day only lasts for a few moments until I find ways to pick myself apart." Idealists desire to be better, and to become better every day. But who told them this is what they have to live up to? Taking steps every day to become a better person is something we can all do a little more often, but for an Idealist, it may be worth taking a break from this for a while. Whether someone told them that they needed to be better or this is something they've always just told themselves, I think it might be time for some

Idealists to raise their hands and take themselves out of the race for never-ending improvement. I want to be clear that I'm not suggesting you shouldn't take time to improve yourself, but most Idealists will never be satisfied with their continual improvement. Striving for better can almost become an addiction for them, and so it's vital for Idealists to step back and realize, yes, I can work to improve myself, but it's not a race. It's not a race with someone else, and it's not a race with myself. I'm allowed to just be.

Spend Time Journaling

I think the ritual of journaling is beneficial for every Enneagram type, but I think it is almost necessary for an Idealist in terms of optimal self-care. Being able to visually see any negative thoughts that have been circling around in your mind or harsh criticisms you may have made about yourself within the privacy and security journaling affords can help you shatter the negative lens through which you've learned to see yourself over the years. Idealists are usually aware that they are hard on themselves, but journaling allows them to better see the often cruel reality of their inner dialogue. I'm sure if others heard the way they beat themselves up inside, they would be heartbroken for the beloved Idealists in their lives. Journaling promotes self-compassion and reflection for a Type 1. It also plays into the nostalgia they so enjoy. Think of journaling as an investment in what will live as a time capsule for your betterment and self-growth.

Communicate and Confide

One of the hardest things for Idealists to practice is confiding in others about their authentic emotions. Communicating in this way is often difficult for Idealists because it typically means they will need to take ownership of their emotions. For example, Idealists recognize when others do wrong, and they know when they're annoyed with others for doing wrong, but vocalizing these thoughts and feelings forces Idealists to see how they may also be contributing to the problem, or how they, too, have made a mistake. But the self-care and self-growth challenge I have for Idealists is to not just communicate to others when you are annoyed with them but confide in others when you feel grief, sadness, joy, and confusion, too. Communicate to others when you are feeling a wide range or mix of emotions. Verbally process with someone you feel safe with, and talk things out with them. I know they will feel so honored to be considered trustworthy in your eyes, and doing this will also promote healthier emotional processing habits for you both. One of my Idealist friends once called me in tears as I was roaming the aisles of Hobby Lobby, and it stopped me in my tracks. She wasn't usually one to be so emotionally available and open, and so I just decided to be there for her as she cried for as long as she needed to. It was a moment in our friendship that I will cherish forever, not because I wanted to see my dear Idealist in pain, but because I could tell this was necessary for her healing. None of us can escape our desire to belong and be loved by others. So communicate when you need love and when you need space. Confide in others, and learn with them, too.

HOW TO TAKE CARE OF
THE TYPE 1 IN YOUR LIFE

Remind Them They Don't Have to
Conquer the World in One Day

If you have a Type 1 in your life, you know that they are extremely reliable and dutiful individuals. They desire to be perfect, and this desire can exhaust them due to their innate drive to fulfill their responsibilities. Idealists want more freedom, they want more balance, they want more control, and they want to save the world from everything that is wrong with it—and they believe it all has to be done not just in their lifetime but sometimes in just twenty-four hours. We admire our wonderful Idealists for being so committed to and brave in their beliefs, and sometimes that can lead us to think they enjoy being responsible all of the time because they seem to be handling everything so well. We've tried to help when we've sensed they might be overloading themselves with responsibility, but there's a certain way they want things to be done, and they're too scared to let us do it. So if they're not letting you help, and you don't want to step on their toes, what are you to do? Well, the first thing you can do for your Idealist is show up for them. Show up with a presence that is ready to welcome their emotional honesty, and remind them that it is not up to them to save the world. They do not have to conquer everything in a day. Reminding them of this is extremely important as the spouse, partner, close family member, or friend of an Idealist. Idealists genuinely often forget it. Sometimes the most helpful thing you can do for them is to let them know they are not alone, that you're present in this situation with them, and that you want to help. Showing them you don't want them to carry the burden alone, while remaining kind and gentle during times of stress, will help them remember that this really wasn't meant for them to endure on their own.

Let Them Be

Idealists need more alone time and time to process than we think. So when I say letting them be is loving them well, I mean it. When they finally give themselves the space to do nothing and relax, release the pressure from them by taking some of their perceived responsibilities off their plate. Do the dishes, keep things clean, fulfill a responsibility that you know you can do well without them having to ask you— Idealists are all about seeing that you care about them through your actions, so as they are enjoying their alone time, show them in the aftermath that you are trustworthy, and that they can take breaks and time to themselves more often. Letting them be without adding any pressure, or keeping all potential distractions or interruptions away from them during their alone time, will mean so much more to them than you could ever know!

Celebrate Good Times

As I mentioned throughout this chapter, learning how to celebrate themselves and their life freely, without feeling the need to earn it, is a great way for Idealists to practice self-care and grow as humans. Whether you're a spouse, partner, family member, or friend, helping your sweet Idealist celebrate simply for the purpose of celebrating will show you care deeply about them. So try brightening or celebrating their day by buying them their favorite chocolate, or finally watching that movie they've been wanting to see. Or maybe, come home with flowers or another token of gratitude they'd appreciate after a long day of work. Make them a playlist of happy music that they can crank up at any given moment throughout their day. Throw them a party for their half birthday or plan their dream vacation, where they won't have to worry about a single detail—anything to help them remember that life isn't just about measuring your work ethic, measuring your integrity, or just measuring things in general; it's about living. It's about loving. It's about enjoying.

THE HELPER

GENEROUS, SINCERE, FRIENDLY,
POSSESSIVE, WARMHEARTED

CORE DESIRES:
To be worthy of love, to be wanted,
to be thought of by others as irreplaceable

CORE FEARS:
Being unlovable,
replaceable, undesirable

ULTIMATE MOTIVATIONS:
To love and feel love deeply, to show their
affection and feelings to others, to feel validated
and needed by others, to experience a mutual
emotional response and connection

AFFIRMATION:
"I am wanted."

Enneagram Type 2s are often referred to as the "helpers" of our world. They are the ones who walk into a room and can immediately sense what everyone needs. They are the friends that always remember your birthday and show up to support you no matter what, and they usually struggle with people-pleasing. They are naturally inclined toward living a life filled with relational connection, however they define or see relational connection being important. Living their life to the fullest means sacrificing their own needs for the needs of others and making sure that others find them irreplaceable. At the end of the day, Helpers are always pursuing what will make others feel loved, as well as what will make them feel appreciated. While all Type 2s show up as "helpers" in life, every Type 2 has a different idea of what "help" looks like to them, personally. That being said, they will always strive to be your friend and be there for you no matter what, although they sometimes can lose their identity in this pursuit.

You Might Be a Helper If . . .

- You can walk into a room and immediately pick up on everyone's emotions whether or not you personally know any of the people.
- You tend to know what someone needs before that person even knows it. But if someone were to ask you what you need, you would have no clue how to answer.
- You prioritize your relationships and friendships over work most of the time. It feels selfish to do otherwise.
- When someone is confiding in you about something, you may not remember to listen to them before offering

your opinion or advice because you feel as though you already know what they need.

- Although you consider yourself to be a selfless person, you tend to help others with the secret hope they will offer you some type of friendship or emotional connection in return. When they don't extend that to you, you can become frustrated and hurt.
- Being with people and having a close circle of friends fulfills you most.
- Even if you may not like to admit it, words of affirmation and external validation from those you consider important are extremely meaningful for you to receive. It just feels so good to be loved.
- You take criticism very personally. You can't stand receiving harsh or inconsiderate feedback.
- It really bothers you when people don't say "thank you" or notice all of the hard work you or others are putting in behind the scenes.
- You have let people take advantage of your time and energy in the past, but you didn't realize it at the time because you genuinely wanted to be helpful and a good friend.
- You have neglected physical, emotional, or spiritual needs of your own in order to care for the physical, emotional, and spiritual needs of someone else.

2W1 2s who lean into their 1 wing are a little less outgoing and a little more unassuming than 2W3s. They desire to meet the needs of others, but do so quietly, in an orderly manner, and behind the scenes. They feel like receiving affirmation and gratitude for their actions is selfish, and they keep many of their emotional impulses in check in order to be a "good" spouse, employee, friend, parent, or child. These 2s are heartfelt, sincere, and purposeful. You are probably unaware of all that they do for you on a daily basis, and they probably are resisting telling you about it. If you have a special person who's a Type 2 in your life, sit them down and give them a back rub or a big hug. They deserve it.

2W3 2W3s are more outgoing and image conscious than 2W1s. These 2s love to be "in the know"—whether that's regarding the lives of others or the latest trends. They are not just trying to be a lovable, caring presence; they are trying to be the *most* lovable and caring presence, the best of best friends. They strive to be on top of all their relationships and believe that love is earned through relational achievements, which means they have a harder time recognizing when they're being taken advantage of. These 2s are a little more emotionally expressive, and they seriously desire deep, meaningful relationships, but often lose themselves in this pursuit. If you have a 2W3 in your life, draw back the curtain and check in on how they are feeling. Help them slow down, and vocally affirm them about things that have nothing to do with their performance. Thank them for their hard work, and give them the space to just be.

WHY HELPERS NEED SELF-CARE

Enneagram Type 2s seek friendship, relationships, and connection above all else, and sometimes at the cost of their own health and well-being. Helpers tend to identify themselves so heavily with their relationships that they will often refer to themselves in relation to someone else, such as the spouse, partner, best friend, or assistant, rather than addressing who they are apart from those relationships. They ultimately desire to be irreplaceable to those they care about in their life, and this desire can sometimes cause them to miss out on the self-expression and passion that lies within them, even if it does require saying no to someone or something they love. They can end up living frivolous, messy, and abusive lives if they do not take care of themselves. 2s, you need self-care so that you can actually help others generously and selflessly, while also experiencing a life full of creativity and self-love. Through the practice of self-care and reflection, the Helper will discover that being wanted or needed by others does not give them their ultimate value. In fact, they will become more individualistic and emotionally honest individuals.

SELF-CARE PRACTICES FOR TYPE 2S

Say No

One way Helpers can practice better self-care is by learning it's okay to say no. Many Helpers often find themselves overcommitted and spread too thin in their life. When someone asks them for a favor, or they see someone who looks like they need help, Helpers are always ready to step up to the plate. Their generosity is honorable, but sometimes it can become excessive. When they've given too much of their time, resources, and energy, they risk becoming burnt out and angry. Angry that they couldn't help themselves. Angry that no one thanked them. But even when they're burnt out, they keep going. It's hard for a Helper to recognize when they need to say no and slow down, but it is necessary for their self-care. A few things all Helpers should know: You're allowed to say that little word—"No." You're allowed to say, "Can I get back to you tomorrow?" You're allowed to say, "Let me think about it and I will let you know." These words often feel too risky. Maybe you fear saying it not because you're afraid you'll be replaced, but because you're afraid of the emotions that might arise when you do. But that's all the more reason why you should begin practicing saying "no." Start by saying no to small things, such as another night of having people over at your house. Saying no to reaching out to others all the time. Saying no to replying to texts or emails right away. As you work your way up to saying no to bigger things, notice how your value doesn't come from what you agreed or declined to do, but from who you are.

Question Your Emotions

Helpers can pick up on the emotions of others very easily—in fact, other people's emotions are contagious for Helpers—meaning most Helpers can mistake someone else's feelings as their own because they care so much about how the other person feels in the moment. Although this amazing empathy is an admirable quality to have, when it is left unchecked, it can lead Helpers to develop a false perception of their internal reality. Helpers will begin to believe they are okay or not okay based upon whatever emotional burden they are helping to carry for someone else at the time. What also causes Helpers to suppress their authentic feelings is that they often experience an intense inner conflict when their emotions are at odds with those of someone they love. This is why it's so important for Helpers to take a step back and think about how they feel about any emotional situation they're involved in. Think: Am I happy just because this other person is happy? Am I feeling anxious just because this other person is? Getting in touch with yourself through those self-reflective questions will allow Helpers to be there for their loved ones with both empathy and better emotional stability. It will allow them to reconcile their inner conflict and be true to their authentic emotional experience without shame.

Awaken Your Inner Artist

Almost every Type 2 I've met has had a penchant for crafting and is fluent in the language of DIY. This is to say they're incredibly innovative, although they might not see themselves as such because of how easily it comes to them. It's hard for them to justify pursuing their creative passion because it interferes with the role they play in other people's lives. It's relatively easy for a Helper to be influenced by the opinions and preferences of everyone else, and when one of their more individualistic desires is brought into question by someone they admire, it can be hard for them to stand up for themselves. But the truth is, engaging in their creative pursuits is one of the most revitalizing and refreshing activities for their soul. Helpers have beautiful minds that long for somewhere to pour out all of their deep insights. By awakening their inner artist, they will begin to see how their value to the world goes beyond how they can help and what they can give, and extends into what they create, dream up, and imagine—not just for others but for themselves.

Call Your Best Friend

One of the most therapeutic things Helpers can do for themselves is chat with their closest, dearest friend without any time constraint. Healthy, thriving friendships are very important to Type 2s, and making sure their best friend is safe, well-loved, and taken care of genuinely brings them joy. That's why, if it is not already in your self-care routine, prioritizing talks with your best friend is important for you as a Helper—and especially for your mental health. Prioritize those talks even when you're the one in need of support. Even when you're struggling. Call and talk about your day, whether it's good or bad, and choose to believe that you are not a burden. You would never view your best friend's struggles, vents, or problems as burdens, so why would they think that about you? In fact, I can guarantee your BFF is waiting for you to open up to them a little bit more; to not be only the one asking the questions and fulfilling the needs, but also the one who answers, the one you listen to, the one who asks for prayer or help. The people in your life, especially your best friend, genuinely want to support you as much as you support them, so allow them to show up for you on both the good days and bad. Call your best friend!

Tell Others What You Need

Helpers have a distinct, almost psychic, ability to immediately know what another person may need. That's why a lot of Helpers find themselves in careers involving counseling, assisting, or taking care of others in some way: they intuitively can piece together what someone else may need because of how deeply they feel. Helpers don't realize that this is a unique ability they possess, and that not everyone can pick up on the things that come so naturally to them. They are wanted and needed often because of this ability—it makes them irreplaceable in situations of chaos or crisis. Where the problem begins to develop for them is when *they* start to need something . . . and no one recognizes they are in need (because, unfortunately, the rest of us don't have your superpower!). Helpers tend to take it personally when others haven't picked up on what they need, and can sometimes even hold this against them. They become irritable and frustrated, feeling as though no one is ever going to take care of them in the way they take care of others. The truth is, though, because we can't practically read others' minds like you can, most of the people in your life genuinely don't know you need something because you haven't told them. Helpers, I know what you may be thinking right now: "I *shouldn't* have to tell them." Even if you believe this, though, you have to understand that most people do in fact have to communicate to others when they need something. The person you're waiting to take care of you may never realize they should because you haven't said as much. Or because you've said you're fine over and over again. I'm not saying this is fair, but you have to remember that in any healthy friendship or relationship, it's important to speak up about what you need. If you continue to believe that other people can read your mind like you can theirs, you're only going to be disappointed. So what do you need, dear Helper? Think about it. Really think about it. And then tell somebody!

Use Essential Oils

When Helpers practice better self-care and begin to take steps toward self-growth, they become more awakened and creative individuals. I think a fun way for a Helper, regardless of gender or age, to use this creativity is through essential oils. The reason I think this would be beneficial to a Helper specifically is that with essential oils they have the freedom to create their own unique combination of aromas. Whether they have only a few different types of oils in their possession or an entire kit, personalizing the scent of every room in their house by mixing and matching the oils can help restore a Helper's soul. Not only would they be tapping into their artistic nature but they'd also be creating a home that is unique and nurturing in how it welcomes others in. Their house will have a distinct essence and scent that will envelop their friends and family as soon as they walk through the front door. Helpers can also use essential oils to create their own signature perfume or soap scent. This playful experimentation, whether it's with essential oils or aromatherapy, is a wonderful way for Helpers to take care of themselves and their already welcoming spaces.

You're Allowed to Be Supported

As I mentioned earlier, Helpers have a hard time letting others support them. To say accepting support feels deeply selfish to them is an understatement—asking someone else for help, or crying on someone's shoulder, means that Helpers would have to admit they need something, and as you well know, they would rather not have to admit it. Helpers believe their sole purpose is essentially to be at the service of others, and they take great pride in that, though it may not be readily apparent. Many of us don't pick up on Type 2s' sense of pride because to appear selfish or self-centered in any fashion would feel like the end of the world to a Helper. But the truth is, Helpers, you're allowed to be the shoulder to cry on, while also crying on someone else's. You're allowed to give, and you're allowed to take. You're allowed to give advice, and you're allowed to receive it. You don't have to be everything to everyone—because you're worth so much more than that. You have your own heart, soul, mind, and desires that deserve to be supported and cheered for by others! It doesn't make you selfish, it makes you human. You can't believe no one wants to support you if you're not letting people in to know that you want their support! It's okay to ask. So many people are waiting to root for you, to cry with you, to give the hug you're always giving. It's time to receive, my love. Let yourself receive.

Rest Up, Buttercup!

Do you know what sounds like hell for an Enneagram Type 2? Doing nothing alone. That's right: Not completing a task, not putting something on their plate, not showing up for someone, not inviting someone over—doing nothing while being alone might even be the thing that Helpers avoid the most in life. But while they avoid it, it is one of the most beneficial things they can do for their mental health. Just like the rest of us, Helpers need rest. They need time, space, and solitude. They need bubble baths, face masks, Netflix, and *actual* chill. They need their phones on "Do Not Disturb" mode. They need it as much as anyone else, and Helpers hate admitting that. Remember, lovely Helpers, that the more time you take for yourself to recharge and refresh, the more internal love and kindness you will be able to give to yourself and to those you care about. So what brings you rest? I want you, as a Helper, to sit back, set the book down for a moment, and think about this question honestly. Now grab a journal or open the Notes app on your phone and compile a list of things that make you feel whole and well-rested. After you've written them down, share that list with someone. Talk about it with them. Allow them to help you set up a plan of action, so you can begin to incorporate more rest in your day-to-day routine. Maybe this entails shutting off your email at a certain time of day. Maybe it's choosing a set time to do yoga outside in the mornings. Whatever it is, find what works best for you, and then do it without shame! You deserve to rest up.

Give Anonymously

Helpers usually give the best gifts. It's true. They have a remarkable ability to know exactly what you want, which makes the holiday season sacred for them. Seeing their family and friends open up gifts they've bought them makes Helpers so inexplicably happy. But often, Helpers secretly want to receive affirmations from their loved ones *because* they gave them gifts—rather than receiving a gift in return. Helpers want to hear, "You're my best friend," "You're the best partner," or "What would I do without you?" But a great self-growth and self-care practice for a Helper is to try giving gifts anonymously—and not only to loved ones. Helpers, whenever you give to organizations or charity, refrain from telling anyone you've done so. This will begin to create a genuine selfless-ness within you, rather than prop up an artificial one. Helpers may find themselves more fulfilled from this kind of gift-giving as well because they are learning to find satisfaction and validation within themselves, rather than from external relationships.

Find a Favorite Coffee Shop

A fun, simple act of self-care for a Helper is to find a favorite coffee shop. So, Helpers, hop in your car, on your own, and venture out into your city or the surrounding areas. Try out a few different coffee shops until you find the one—the place that sells your favorite mocha or latte, the one that has the velvet seat by the front windows where the sun shines across your face in the best way, where you can comfortably people-watch from the inside and outside, where you can easily daydream. Learn the names and stories of the baristas. Invite old and new friends to sit and talk with you for hours at your favorite booth or table. Having favorite places to visit in your city warms your soul like nothing else. Helpers are incredible hosts and hostesses; they bring people together in a way that is heartfelt and unique. Finding their coffee shop, I think, is a small but beneficial step Helpers can take to bring themselves joy.

Enjoy Nature Solo

Helpers love nature. Whether they appreciate nature through hiking, surfing, and relaxing outdoors or buying fresh flowers and produce from the farmers' market, Helpers are often very interested in things that better connect them to our planet. Settling into a self-care rhythm that continually allows them to take part in these nature-loving experiences during whatever season of life they're in will only help enhance their journey toward self-discovery. The key to getting the most out of these experiences, however, is for a Helper to do them alone. Although it may be challenging for you as a Helper, going on a hike without engaging in a conversation or making sure everyone has water and snacks is essential for you to freely enjoy your surroundings. When you spend alone time in nature, you can observe and experience it in any way you desire. Take your time with it. Go to the spots where you want to go, and not where you think everyone else would want to go. Take notes on and pictures of what you like—free from the distraction of other people's needs and input and preferences. It's so important for Helpers to allow themselves to enjoy life and experiences in the way *they* want to—because this will allow them to grow into more fulfilled and content individuals.

Take Yourself on a Date

Helpers make phenomenal partners. Being sacrificial and loving in relationships comes naturally to them, and receiving that romantic type of love from someone else is something they deeply desire. Most Helpers I've met have desired to be in a relationship with someone from a young age. The thought of such an intense connection and partnership is so appealing to them that they want to jump into dating someone as soon as they can. Helpers can find themselves quickly developing crushes and dreaming of the day when they're no longer single, and they typically want everyone they meet to fall in love with them (secretly, of course). Even when their feelings may not be reciprocated, they take that as a personal challenge and try to find a way to prove that they're worthy of the other person's love. Many of the Helpers I know have had their time, energy, and emotions taken advantage of in relationships, simply because Helpers want to care for others well, and to be cared for in return. The thing is, Helpers deserve so much more than this. They deserve the same, or an even stronger, amount of thoughtfulness from people they care about. They deserve to know their worth—and to recognize when someone is not treating them the way they should be treated. So whether or not you're in a relationship, I want you, sweet Helper, to take yourself out on a date for a change—and not just any date: the date you deserve. The date you dream of and fantasize about. Show yourself you're worthy of that kind of treatment whether or not you have a special someone in your life to give it to you.

Let Others Reach Out

I would say most Helpers are known for initiating conversation with their loved ones. They keep a mental checklist of who they need to make sure is okay at any given point in time, and they frequently like to reach out to others to see how they're doing. This can create an imbalance early on in a Helper's friendships or relationships, because everyone then expects the Helper to always reach out first. However, the Helper may become upset or feel as though no one cares how they're doing because they don't give others the opportunity to reach out to them. As a self-care exercise to remedy this issue, I want you, as a Helper, to do a little cleanse. Take a week off from reaching out. I mean it. Don't text anyone first, don't reach out to anybody just to check in on them, and see what happens. You may be surprised by how many or how few friends reach out. Although that may be hard for you, I believe it's important for Helpers to know which friends are as invested in their friendship as they are. You deserve to have friends in your life who value your relationship and understand you are more than what you give. Let others reach out to you first.

Find Pen Pals

Helpers love meeting new people and making new friends, and they always remember meaningful details from the stories people tell them. Helpers genuinely adore learning about the lives of others, and they relish connecting with all sorts of individuals regardless of their background, gender, or age. It brings them joy and makes life richer for them. I think a fun, unique way for Helpers to really lean into this love for conversation and getting to know people on a deeper level is by getting a few pen pals from other cities and countries. There are a lot of amazing websites that provide a safe way to exchange letters with others around the globe, and being able to learn how other people love, feast, celebrate, mourn, survive, and live their life will inspire Helpers to break out of their comfort zone as well. A wonderful way for Helpers to nourish their soul is by creating a large, loving community that crosses borders and oceans, and having pen pals from faraway places will give Helpers the special opportunity to get to know someone's heart without being able to observe or interact with them in person. I know Helpers would cherish the experience, as well as enjoy this creative exchanging of emails or letters!

Write Love Letters to Yourself

I'd be shocked if you've never received a "just because" text, call, or card in the mail from a Helper in your life. Helpers are always thinking of how someone else needs to be reminded of how much they're loved, and doing so brings them a lot of joy and satisfaction. As Helpers continue to cheer on others in their life, I want to add one more person to their list of who they should send a "just because" type of message: themselves. I want them to write a love letter or a hype-up text addressed to themselves and then literally send it to themselves to read. What Helpers may not realize is that underneath their innate desire to always be encouraging others, they're secretly seeking that from others as well. But it's okay to admit to yourself, "I really need someone to encourage me right now." It's okay if that person is a close friend or family member, and it's okay if that person is you! Helpers' covert reliance on others for encouragement can lead to frequent disappointment and failed expectations, but rather than expecting others to cheer you on, expect it from yourself for a change. Look in the mirror and give yourself that pep talk you want. Say that you're beautiful, loving, kind, and valuable—that you are wanted in this world and in your community, not for what you give but for who you are. You are cherished and respected. You are creative and innovative. You are everything and more, my dear Helper. Hype yourself up. Be confident in the unique soul you've been given.

HOW TO TAKE CARE OF THE TYPE 2 IN YOUR LIFE

Reach Out First

If you have a Type 2 in your life, you know how much they value close, personal friendships. They desire to be wanted by their friends, and this desire can exhaust them due to their innate drive to always be creating deep connections. Helpers want more conversation, they want more relational security, they want more attention, and they want to save and rescue all of their friends from anything that is causing them pain. We admire our wonderful Helpers for being so committed to their relationships and a sense of unity in a time when it feels as though everyone is striving for the opposite. But sometimes that can lead us to believe they always enjoy being the shoulder to cry on or taking care of us. After all, they have a tendency to drop everything and minister to us when we need them. The truth is, while Helpers do love giving themselves and their care to others, they can also grow exhausted from it. They can become tired of keeping the conversation going, or frankly of always initiating the conversation in the first place. They can become tired of everyone relying on them to be everything, because sometimes they don't feel like they can be *everything* in that moment. A Helper is not inclined to tell you this, though, which is why I'm telling you! A simple yet meaningful way you can subtly thank them for being such caring and loving friends is by reaching out to them first. Beat their 10 A.M. "hey, how are you? :)" text. Call them at 1:50 P.M. instead of 2 P.M. because you just couldn't wait the ten minutes to hear their voice and ask about their day. Make the same effort they always make for you; it will mean the world to them.

Ask Them Intentional Questions

When you ask a Helper, "How are you? What do you need?" it means a lot to them, but those two questions can also be frustrating for them to answer. Helpers honest-to-God don't know how they are most of the time or what they really need. They're not deliberately trying to hide how they're feeling from you; they just genuinely don't know what to say in response. A Helper's mental energy revolves around thinking about everyone else as well as what everyone else thinks of them. When they've finally slowed down to the point where they can hear you ask them how they are doing, they have an emotional breakdown of sorts—because all of their emotions and the emotions of others have been held tight inside them for so long. Rather than jumping into a deep conversation with a Helper with those two questions, try asking something a little more intentional, like "On a scale of one to ten, how stressed would you say you are right now?" or "How would you describe to me how you're feeling today?" or "What are some things you've been thinking about lately?" These more straightforward questions will unlock a flood of answers from a Helper, so once you've asked them, be prepared to give the Helper your full attention. They *have* to have the space to verbally process everything that's going on inside their minds in order to get to any sort of definitive conclusion, so don't change that about them. Empower them in it. Let them talk in circles, and pay close attention so you can help them get where they need to land. Don't tell them how they should be feeling. Ask questions, and let them process until they reach their own conclusion. Providing this support to them emotionally and relationally will skyrocket their self-growth and make them feel like it's okay to take care of themselves.

Plan or Do Something Meaningful for Them

Helpers are always thinking of the next outing to plan with you or gift they want to surprise you with. They love making you feel loved, and seeing you happy makes them happy. If Helpers are honest, though, it's hard for them to not expect the same level of detail and thoughtfulness from you when they reach milestones or achieve things in their lives. However, they'd feel incredibly guilty voicing this struggle of theirs, so they don't do it. You may have even found that your Helper friend has become upset with you in the past because you didn't get them something they never mentioned they were interested in receiving. While communication is of course a two-way street, one way that you can love your Helper well is by stepping into their shoes and tapping into their emotional intuitiveness. Ask more questions, and actively think of them throughout your day. Then plan something for them out of the blue, or surprise them at home with a few of their favorite things. Helpers don't want you to know that they want the same level of thoughtfulness from you, so surprising them with it, and using your actions and time to show how much you care, will make them feel so loved and valued by you.

TYPE 3

THE ACHIEVER

VERSATILE, MOTIVATED,
INFLUENTIAL, CHARMING

CORE DESIRES:

To feel important, invaluable, and successful

CORE FEARS:

Being worthless, humiliated,
unimportant, seen as a "loser"

ULTIMATE MOTIVATIONS:

To be affirmed as individuals and to be affirmed in
their pursuits, to be seen as admirable and impressive
in the eyes of others, to be the center of attention,
to be everything they portray themselves to be

AFFIRMATION:

"I am always worthwhile."

Enneagram Type 3s are often referred to as the "achievers" and "influencers" of our world. They are the ones who walk into a room and can immediately become whoever it is they need to be for the people involved. They are the friends you always go to for career advice, they empower you and make you feel like you can achieve anything, and they are usually terrified of failure and embarrassing themselves in front of others. They are naturally inclined toward living a life of success, however they define or see that success. Living their life to the fullest means striving toward the principles, achievements, and milestones that impress the people from whom they seek approval. I have named them the Achievers, rather than Influencers, because though they heavily influence our society, they base their value on their achievements more than anything else. What may be successful to others may not be what the Type 3 authentically wants to achieve; therefore, being successful completely depends on each individual 3 and what their personal goals are. They will avoid being seen as a failure at all costs, and they sometimes can portray a put-together image even when they are far from it.

You Might Be an Achiever If . . .

- You find yourself drawn to leaders or people of influence in your community and around the world.
- You can easily shape-shift into whatever you think others want you to be when you enter a room.
- You find it very difficult to detach your personal identity from what you produce at work and how you perform.
- When different friend groups meet for the first time,

it really stresses you out because each friend group typically knows only one side of you.

- You are extremely adaptable and you know how to put your feelings aside in order to get a job done.
- You are goal-oriented and like to keep track of how much progress you're making in life, in work, and in relationships.
- You have a tendency to push yourself really hard for a while, and then you completely veg out or go on autopilot until you recover.
- Constantly juggling a million different ideas and projects, you are fueled and also very stressed out by the amount of work you put on your plate.
- Seeing your loved ones live out their dreams and succeed makes you the happiest person in the world. You genuinely just want what's best for them always!
- You have sometimes exaggerated or lied about your authentic self in order to be more acceptable or likable to a certain person or group of people.
- Sometimes you're not even sure what you want to do with your life; you've come so far, but is this what you really want? Or is it what others wanted for you?

3W2 These 3s are energetic and incredible at networking. All strangers are simply friends they haven't met yet, and they make connections with ease. They like to appear put together and are cheerleaders for their friends and family at heart. But these 3s can often lose themselves and their identity in the pursuit of their goals and relationships. More prone to people-pleasing, they have a hard time figuring out what they truly want to pursue, not just what they're expected to pursue. Ultimately, 3W2s help us move forward, reach goals, and make lasting friendships. Encourage them to slow down every now and then and let their hair down, and help them express their deep emotions.

3W4

Type 3s who lean into their 4 wing tend to be more reserved and sensitive. They like to be trendy, but also trendy in a way that's unique. They're more likely to pursue deeper meanings and find hidden emotional patterns in life—and since they believe authenticity is cool, they desire to be authentically successful. These 3s are hard on themselves, often feeling like they are lacking in some substantial way, which causes them to take on much more than they can handle. They usually have a smaller group of friends and are more likely to disappear from them from time to time. These 3s help us find beauty in the midst of our purpose and our setbacks. 3W4s are loyal and care deeply about their work and relationships. If you have one in your life, remind them that when they take the time to just *be*, your love for them won't go away!

WHY ACHIEVERS NEED SELF-CARE

Enneagram Type 3s seek likability and value above all else, sometimes at the cost of being connected to their true self and true emotions. They ultimately want to have the attention and admiration of those in their world, and this desire can sometimes cause them to miss out on the to-getherness and steadiness that already surrounds them, even if it doesn't involve what they deem to be "successful." They can end up living overly planned, disconnected, and superficial lives if they do not take care of themselves. Type 3s, you need self-care so that you can actually achieve your personal goals and aspirations, while also experiencing life and your community fully as your authentic self. Through the practice of self-care and reflection, Achievers will discover that they are not defined by their milestones or their peers. In fact, they will become more community-oriented and grounded individuals.

SELF-CARE PRACTICES FOR TYPE 3S

You May Never Get Someone's Approval, and That's Okay

What people misunderstand about Achievers is that there is always one person or a group of people whom they want to care about them more than anything else. It's easy for Type 3s to dedicate their time to becoming experts at things they think people want them to be experts at. They ride the escalator of success that they're placed on by others or by themselves, but it sucks the passion out of everything they do. It also takes a toll on their self-esteem. That is, although Type 3s may seem really self-assured on the outside, underneath that layer of confidence is the insecurity of not being enough—the feeling that they're meant only to achieve and be approved by others. But, Achievers, I want you to know that you *are* talented, and that it's also okay to *think* you're talented. It's okay to think that what you offer is valuable. And that approval? That affirmation? It may never come. You may never hear that particular person give you the "yes" or the "wow" you're looking for, and that's okay, too. The second you stop living for others' admiration and approval is the second you'll truly start to live, so let yourself be free, friend.

Strive for Average

Achievers desire to be the best at everything they do and revered for their achievements. They want people to ask, "How do they manage to do it all so well?" While these are innately self-centered things to want, they are rooted in a deep sense of insecurity that lies within an Achiever's soul. Achievers need to constantly hear that they're good, that they're the best, and to feel like those things are true even if they aren't, because this sense of purpose and status is where they tend to find most of their identity. When someone challenges one of their abilities, even if the Achiever doesn't have a particular passion for it, they will switch gears and try to become the best at it simply because they need to prove the other person wrong. But, my darling Achievers, when does it stop? When does striving to be the best finally reach its limit? What if you never reach the level you were hoping to reach? Does that mean you're less worthy and less than? What would happen if you strove to be average? The answer is that you would be so confident in your self-worth without the validation of being good at that one random thing—because, honestly, who cares if you're average at that one random thing anyway. Entertain the idea of being average in the things you care about. Why? Because your value is not defined only by your performance in life. If you want to be a successful dancer, you don't need to become the best graphic designer. If you want to be a doctor, you don't have to be the best gymnast. I know that sounds silly, but really think about it. Strive to be average, and know that the love from others won't go away.

Create Inspiring Routines

Because Achievers are prone to overworking themselves, this can cause them to go on autopilot when they are stressed. Their original hunger and drive turns robotic as they naturally grow more concerned about progress and numbers, and they eventually begin to lose all wonder and passion for what they're doing. Achievers can even feel this way for years on end because, despite losing the inspiration they may have had at the start, they don't know how to stop *going* and *doing*. This habit is ultimately unsustainable for Achievers because they're not at their best when they're solely concerned about advancement they can easily measure. But healthy Achievers realize that prioritizing inspiration in their work is important for their self-growth. This is why I encourage all Achievers to create routines that help them strike or reignite inspiration. Block out time to read books, go on Pinterest, watch Netflix, learn about something new, explore a new place in town, and don't share what you're learning or experiencing with anyone else. Keep it sacred. Let yourself marinate in it for an extended period of time before creating something with it. Let yourself be inspired without feeling like you have to take action with it. Create something new without showing it to others. You'll find the work more fulfilling when you do.

Cry It Out

My husband's and my engagement was the worst three months of our life, but I didn't let anyone think that it was. I had this dream expectation of what I thought that time would be like for me, and it was completely shattered by the reality of when different opinions, hurtful pasts, and hard realities all came together at once. Not to mention that I was taking a fully loaded semester as a senior in college. I reached a moment during the engagement when I told my mom, "Plan the wedding. I don't care who's there and I don't care what the colors are. I'm going to get a 4.0 this semester, and that's all that I care about." Around that same time, I had also decided to start an inspirational, faith-focused Instagram account for young women because I was just trying to create something that didn't feel like an absolute failure. Everything was crumbling for me, so I dove headfirst into my assignments, headfirst into this Instagram account, and did not want to come up for air. Even if I was broken inside, everyone was going to think I simultaneously planned a wedding, made the president's list at my university, and went viral. I was protecting this false sense of control and self because I thought that was what every-one wanted me to do. I put the pressure of being the "successful one" on myself in the midst of it all, when in reality, I was just running from so much pain I didn't want to feel. And I fully convinced myself that I was fine. Until one day as one of my bridesmaids and I were talking about everything going on, my body just kind of gave up. I started having a panic attack, which I also was trying to control, and she could see it in my face. I remember her looking me in the eyes and saying, "Christina, you're not loved any less if you're broken right now." And man, that did it for me. I began bawling my eyes out as I fell into my dear friend. Achievers, I tell this story because I know you would rather not share those moments of helplessness with people, even if that's maybe what others are wanting from you. But there's probably an intense feeling inside you right now that you're so detached from that you don't even realize it's there anymore, and sometimes crying is a good way to reconnect with that. This is vitally important for you to do as part of your self-care practice because you're not any less loved if you're broken right now. You're not any less loved if you can't keep working. You're not any less loved if you don't even know why you need to cry. So just cry it out. It's okay.

Devote Yourself to Real Authenticity

When they're in an unhealthy state, Achievers are prone to being incredibly narcissistic. The reason for this being that Achievers, though they may not seem like it, are actually highly emotional beings. They are constantly retaining and processing the emotions of others around them as they strive to be unaffected by them. But sometimes, the people they love or admire expect an emotional response from them, and Achievers can seem incredibly emotional and authentic in the moment, even when they are not. The scariest part of this is, a lot of Achievers don't even realize they engage with this false sense of feeling. The speed at which a Type 3 can suppress their emotions is unmatched. But because Achievers still want to be who people expect and admire, they perform, in a way. You're emotionally there, but you're not *actually* there. This can be extremely hurtful and confusing to so many other types, and many Achievers don't even realize they're engaging in this behavior. Chances are, Achievers aren't doing this intentionally. The pace they function at is so fast that it takes a long time for them to process what's happening and how they feel about it. If you're an Achiever and can relate to every-thing I'm saying, I want to challenge you to devote yourself to real authenticity—not the authenticity you think everyone wants from you—and to really feel and share the actual raw, ugly emotions you're experiencing on the inside. I mean it when I say it's an Achiever's life's work; it won't get easier, but you can become more aware.

Create Rhythms of Rest

I say this on behalf of everyone who knows you and loves you, my dear: you seriously have to chill. Achievers are never not moving, doing, working, or hustling. They have tons of ideas, oodles of visions, and they work until their bodies won't let them anymore. Achievers were either brought up to believe or were born with this sense that they have to earn rest, and this belief is highly toxic to an Achiever because they never feel as though they've earned anything. There are few things they can do to make themselves feel like they've earned the right to let go and do whatever the heck they want, and usually these things take *years* of work. Achievers, you don't need to reach that goal before letting your-self close your laptop. Rest isn't a race, and isn't not a competition—but if it were, the human reality that your body needs rest would win every single time. You're never going to beat it. Achievers can also struggle with believing that they have to "do" rest and relaxation in the best way possible. Why do Achievers let themselves believe this? Life is hard for Type 3s when there isn't a goal or purpose behind what they're doing.

So, to give you Achievers a purpose for slowing down, here's a goal for rest: be a living, breathing human. Yep, that's it. I challenge all Achievers to incorporate a routine of rest into their life. You're allowed to and you must experience it every day, every week, every month. Dressing for success may get you somewhere, but resting for success is what will really help you on your self-care journey as well as in your career.

Laugh at Yourself

Achievers have an intense fear of public humiliation. To them, being embarrassed is the equivalent of dying. Okay, maybe that's a little over-dramatic, but it does feel like that to Achievers sometimes. Depending on the Achiever, they can take teasing or slight jabs pretty personally because of how it could taint their public image. Letting loose and showing others their goofy side is difficult for them. While some people struggle to get serious, Achievers struggle to get silly. I believe that Type 3s are worried about how their humor, or their reaction to some-one else's humor, will come across. When Noah, my husband, and I got married, no one could prepare me for the amount of goofiness I was in for—Noah is one of the funniest people I know, but that was really hard for me to deal with at first because of how tense I constantly was and am. After a while, though, I slowly started to let his jokes break down my walls, and it was honestly one of the best things I've ever done for myself. I want to encourage Achievers to let themselves be laughed at and teased every now and then. I'm serious. Let yourself be roasted. Let yourself be made fun of. Try out a self-deprecating joke. Let your jokes flop. Laugh openly at something you think is funny. Laugh at yourself, more. It's good self-care, I promise.

Intentionally Fail

This is more of a challenge than anything else. I know a lot of Idealists, Challengers, and Individualists will be able to relate to it as well, so they should feel free to heed this advice, too. Achievers are very apprehensive about trying anything that they may not be good at. In fact, if an Achiever is not immediately good at the skill or ability they're trying to acquire, they give up as quickly as they started. The relationship between failure and a Type 3 is tense, and Achievers usually let failure hold the upper hand in their life. But I want to challenge Achievers to take back their inner power because I believe failure is not supposed to sabotage or rule over our lives, no matter who you are. The way Achievers can overcome this fear of failure is by intentionally failing. I'm certain all the Achievers who are reading this just said "Yeah, no" in their minds, but hear me out. When I first saw someone ride a skateboard when I was younger, I immediately wanted to know how to ride a skateboard. Same with horseback riding. And cross-country running. And gymnastics. So I tried all of these things—and failed miserably at them. Once failed, I then quit these activities entirely. I quit because I was humiliated and I didn't want anyone to think of me as lesser. But now, as a twenty-two-year-old, I am learning how to skateboard. You heard me. I'm saying screw it. I've failed and fallen many times, but it's made me resilient. It's made me realize I can do more than just what lies within my natural skill set. So choose something you've always wanted to try, and do it. But don't just do it once, do it a few times. Pick a new thing every month. Fail at it every month. You'll feel the fear of failure slowly losing its grasp on your life.

Tell the Whole Truth

If I'm honest, friends, this advice is the hardest for me to write because of how embarrassed I am by how this issue has been present in my own life. But I'm committed to sharing honest self-care advice for every type, even if it's painful for me to hear. I'm going to just come out and say it: I struggle with lying. When I'm in a state of stress, I struggle with exaggeration. I'm sure many Achievers can relate to this. Once a Type 3 has engaged someone, it can be hard for them to stick to the facts when talking about themselves, because they never want to lose their "audience's" attention or seem unlikable. And I have seen a lot of Achievers, and I know a lot of Achievers, who struggle with this as well: the avoidance of admitting reality or admitting the entire truth of a situation. But, my darling Achievers, this makes you seem untrustworthy. I know that's harsh, but it's the truth. It can make others feel ashamed about where they're at in life because they're comparing their experience to yours, when in reality what you're telling them isn't the whole truth. I want to encourage all Achievers to really dig deep and reflect on when and where you haven't told the whole truth in the past. Are there areas in your life where you're doing that now? Admit it to yourself. Accept it. It does not taint your worthiness, but it's essential for your growth.

Stop Overpromising

Achievers tend to not only spread themselves thin but also drag others into their overpromising. They never want to let anyone down, and they never want to back away from any project that has the chance to further them in their goals. The issue is, they also don't want to turn down the opportunities that may not matter as much to them, because what if someone doesn't like them if they say no? What if that person says bad things about them behind their back, tarnishing their reputation? For most of the Achievers I know, by the time Monday rolls around, the amount of promises they've made to people and the task list that follows are paralyzing. For an Achiever's self-care and mental health, they've got to stop this cycle, because what taints their image more than saying no is saying yes and being untruthful. Saying yes, and then ignoring or ghosting others. Saying yes, and saying that they're so excited, among other phrases they may not mean. The biggest step of growth a Type 3 can take is being aware of this cycle and attempting to really step back and feel everything in the moment. Don't feel like you need to answer nonurgent emails immediately. Take thirty minutes, or even a day, to give an honest answer. I also used to think responding to everyone immediately was better than not responding at all, but sometimes the most authentic thing we can do *is* to not respond. Stop keeping up appearances, and stop overpromising.

Do More For-Fun-Only Things

When Achievers find something they love doing, they immediately begin to think of ways they can either make money off it or impress others with it. I'm just being honest—it's how an Achiever's mind is wired to work. This doesn't always mean Achievers are only in it for the money; they can just misjudge enjoyment for their true calling. Achievers want to make passion purposeful in some way, which is why you see so many influencers streaming themselves while playing video games on Twitch. Really think about it: the chance to be "lazy" and play the game you really want to play, with the potential of making some decent money and gaining more exposure—it's an Achiever's heaven! But I want to challenge Achievers to *just* play the video game they want, or watch that show, or do that thing they feel guilty for doing because it's not productive. Rather than trying to find a way to monetize an activity so you feel less guilty for enjoying it, just let yourself feel what you're feeling. Work through the guilt; recognize why you're feeling it. Name the emotion, accept it, and then move on. Because you're allowed to have things in your life that you enjoy and that are for fun only.

Enforce a Digital Sunset

One of the best self-care decisions I ever made for myself was enforcing a "digital sunset," and I believe many Achievers will find it beneficial as well. Since Achievers are almost always working, you will often find them looking at some sort of electronic device—be it a laptop, iPad, or phone. They have few to no boundaries with technology these days, and it tends to be the main thing that can consume their life and steal their energy. I first heard of the "digital sunset" practice from mental health influencer, advocate, and speaker Mike Foster on an episode of his *Fun Therapy* podcast. He talked about how every night at 8:00, he puts all his devices far out of reach and is not allowed to touch them again until 8:00 the next morning. While this was hard at first, he found that the longer he did it, the better he slept, the better he felt, the more creative he became, and the happier a human being it made him. I wanted to try it as well, and when I committed to doing the "digital sunset" every day for two months, I never felt better. It seriously changed my life. It kept me from getting too sucked into my work, and I believe it will help other Achievers do the same.

Leave Work at Home

As someone who currently works from home, I want to clarify what I mean by the following sentence. Growing up, I always took my homework, extracurriculars, passion projects, and more with me everywhere. I kept them in my purse at all times—at social gatherings, during nights at youth group, on vacations and retreats. Leaving my tasks at home was nearly impossible for me to do, and if you asked anyone I grew up with, they could confirm that this seemed to be my only state of being. I always had to have a goal or my goal always had to be with me. I never just . . . was there. And the truth is, that was my biggest fear. I didn't want to just be there; I wanted to be admirable. I wanted to feel like others loved me and saw how hard I was working, because I wouldn't feel valuable without that affirmation. I know Achievers can relate to this as well, but I think they hate it because it seems purposeless. The truth is, it kind of *is* purposeless, but that's the point. A Type 3's self-care and self-growth work revolves around the acknowledgment that they are worthwhile even when they are achievement-less, that when they're just there—just being—they're full of worth and value and are loved for who they are apart from everything else. So join me, Type 3s, in the commitment to not bring work where it doesn't belong. We can just *be* together.

Live Unfiltered

Take the mask off. Take off the filter. Post an ugly picture. Share an embarrassing moment. Have a dance party with your best friend and let them see you make a fool of yourself in the best way. Be unapologetically goofy. Say the word or words you're too afraid to say. Pursue the things that no one else but you wants to pursue. Post something you're passionate about that also may upset people. Be controversial. Take important stances. Risk the curated image of yourself by sharing what you believe in. Risk being embarrassed by trying to do the seemingly impossible when no one else would. Be free. Listen to the songs that you want to hear. Like the things that you like, not what you're supposed to like. Wear the clothes you like and you think are cool. And if you don't know where to begin with anything that I listed, my dear Achiever, it's time to figure out who you really are, not just who you are in relation to what you're expected to be, or what you're expected to produce for others. Because if you're going to be liked, loved, and admired in this life, don't you want it to be for who you really are?

HOW TO TAKE CARE OF
THE TYPE 3 IN YOUR LIFE

Help Them Let Their Hair Down

If you have a Type 3 in your life, you know how much they value their personal and professional successes. They desire to be worthy of other people's attention, and this desire can exhaust them due to their innate drive to chase whatever they deem worthy enough. Achievers want to make more impact, they want more affirmation, they want more status, and they want to make people they know, as well people they don't, proud of who they are and what they've accomplished. We admire our wonderful Achievers for being so committed to empowerment and influence in a time when it feels as though everyone is striving for the opposite, and sometimes that can lead us to thinking that Type 3s enjoy being the one who is most likely to succeed in the eyes of others. The truth is, while Achievers do love gaining approval and validation, they're also hurting. They're hurting from having to juggle the pressure. They're hurt from everyone assuming they're always going to show up and be the best at whatever is in front of them. They're hurt from everyone always reaching out to them because of what they can offer or *do* for them, and it never being about who they are underneath it all. Because of this, the deepest way you can love your Achiever is by helping them let their hair down. Create an environment where they feel safe enough to leave their appearances and roles outside the door right as they walk in, knowing that when they're with you, there's no performance necessary. They can finally laugh, cry, process, and be who they've been wanting to be all day. The more people an Achiever can feel safe to do this with, the more they'll actually want to explore who they are authentically.

Recognize Their Effort

Achievers are known for creating incredible things, but the most defeating thing for them would be for you to overlook all the effort they actually put into something they've created. Achievers can make things look effortless because that's how they want it to appear to you. But the reality is, the majority of the time, Achievers worked extremely hard to produce the thing they've shown you. They may have endured long, sleepless nights, or said no to friends and experiences and other opportunities in order to finish a project, so when you assume that no work went into what they created, it's actually more anxiety-inducing for them than flattering. They may think you now expect them to effortlessly produce even better work, over and over and over again. So whether you're the spouse, partner, friend, coach, or parent of an Achiever, take the time to celebrate their hard work—not just what they finished but their endurance through it all. This makes an Achiever feel as though they're being loved and appreciated for who they are instead of solely for what they've produced.

Catch Them

Achievers have a hard time balancing lightheartedness and heavy-heartedness, so they often carry both with them at all times. They don't know how people will perceive them in the heavy, and they're unsure of what people will think of them in the light. That's why it feels like Achievers can sometimes say something without really saying anything.

Achievers desperately want to avoid saying or doing the thing that could ruin the love, achievement, or reputation they've worked for, but this cycle is like walking on a never-ending balance beam, and one day, they're going to fall off. Catch them. Help to make things light when they can be light, and encourage an Achiever's silliness and hidden hilarious nature. Then help them accept the heavy; sit in it with them, and let them feel and be overcome by everything going on inside. Catching them and being with them in these moments are acts of kindness you can show Achievers to help them become their most authentic self. They will feel so loved and safe with you because of it.

TYPE 4

THE INDIVIDUALIST

CREATIVE, SELF-AWARE, EMOTIONALLY
HONEST, INSPIRED, AND INSPIRATIONAL

CORE DESIRES:

To be authentically themselves and to
discover what makes them significant

CORE FEARS:

Being without a distinct identity or ordinary

ULTIMATE MOTIVATIONS:

To showcase their individuality, to emotionally
express themselves, to create beautiful
things, to surround themselves with pleasing
aesthetics, to prove their significance

AFFIRMATION:

"I am loved for who I am."

Enneagram Type 4s are often referred to as the "individualists" and "creators" of our world. They are the ones who walk into a room and want to be the most unique and interesting people there. They are the friends you always go to when you need emotional validation. They encourage you to explore the depths of your feelings and usually see themselves as being exceptional (or exceptionally flawed) or different from everyone else. They are naturally inclined toward living a life of self-expression, however they define it. Living their life to the fullest means striving for beauty in their passions and finding out who they really are. I call Types 4s the "Individualists" rather than "Creators" because not all of them are creative in the artistic sense. More than anything, Type 4s simply want to be individualistic, and each Type 4 has a different idea of what that looks like. They are usually rather sensitive and introverted, and they are constantly longing for something they feel is missing in their lives, whether it's a material thing or personal.

You Might Be an Individualist If . . .

- You have always been highly creative and participate in or heavily appreciate the arts.

- Mysteriously, you find something beautiful and exciting about sadness.

- The thought of being "beige" or "average" makes you sick. You're proud to stand out from the crowd.

- Sometimes you go against trends intentionally so that you can continue to differentiate yourself from other people.

- You find joy exploring the depths of your emotions

and human nature, but sometimes you can get stuck in that state of internal questioning and reflecting for long periods of time.

- Your inner dreams and world are extremely vivid. You have an expectation of what you want your life to be, but you don't think you will ever be able to get there.
- Although you don't like to admit it, you feel threatened when someone as unique or inspired as you comes into the picture.
- You have a hard time setting aside your emotions in order to get a job done . . . it just feels inauthentic.
- Sometimes you tend to pull people in very close to you emotionally, but then push them away once they get too close. Even though you don't have a secret, you're afraid of being exposed.
- You feel as though there is something essential lacking in you that everyone else has figured out.
- You have a very specific aesthetic and style, and you like that it distinguishes you from the rest.

4W3
Type 4s who lean into their 3 wing show up in the world as full of wonder and depth as ever. They have big dreams and big passions, and they're going to let you know about them. They're constantly at war with themselves; they feel too much and not enough at the same time. They can take incredible, practical action, but can also fall into a pit of hopelessness in a matter of minutes. They have a secret love for drama—and like to keep life intense.

Although they may be the "happiest" person you know, they have far more complex emotions swirling inside them, and are constantly processing feelings without your knowledge. They truly want to make a memorable impact on the world. If you have a 4W3 in your life, thank them for their passion. Remind them that who they are apart from their dreams and visions matters even more to you.

4W5

4W5s are fascinated by the details and small beauties in life. To them, everything has a deep meaning hidden within it, and they are somewhat addicted to discovering these treasured meanings, especially within themselves and the people they love. These 4s are uncomfortable with the practicalities of life because there seems to be so much more to life than what's on the surface. They are constantly dreaming of having more—better assets, a better self— and can get lost in the pursuit of this in their mind. This also makes them unstoppable visionaries who are unbelievably logical yet also empathetic. If you have a 4W5 in your life, vocally appreciate their unique perspective. They're going to be the ones to sit with you in the darkest of pain. Push them to remember the practical and/or mundane responsibilities of life—like doing the dishes—and show them that they can have all they dream of by taking a few actionable steps.

WHY INDIVIDUALISTS NEED SELF-CARE

Enneagram Type 4s seek authentic identity and self-expression above all else, sometimes at the cost of having consistency and stability. They ultimately desire for their world to be everything they've dreamt of in their minds, and this desire can often keep them from seeing the beauty and opportunities that surround them. They can end up living withdrawn, self-absorbed, and self-destructive lives if they do not take care of themselves. Type 4s, you need self-care so that you can get out of your own way, while also fully experiencing life without feeling like you are flawed. Through the practice of self-care and reflection, Individualists will discover that they are not just defined by what makes them different from others. In fact, they will find that they can be grounded and ambitious people.

SELF-CARE PRACTICES FOR TYPE 4S

Make Your Bed Every Morning

Individualists are daydreamers by nature. They tend to be unmotivated in the face of what they believe are the trivial tasks of life because they think these will distract them from their quest for meaning. But what Individualists don't realize is that while these trivial tasks can be mundane, they play a huge part in their overall mental health. A simple yet effective self-care practice for every Enneagram type, and especially Individualists, is: Before checking your phone or getting started with the day, take a couple of minutes to make your bed. In fact, when you first do it, time yourself. Do this consistently—as much as your life will allow you to— and when you don't feel like making the bed, remember the time it takes to complete the task. Despite everything you may be experiencing internally when you wake up, knowing that making the bed takes only a tiny amount of time will motivate you to just get it done and improve both your mental and physical space. Then try doing this with every task that feels daunting—whether that's checking your emails, answering said emails, or finally doing that workout. Time how long these actions actually take and write down how you felt about doing them afterward. Keep these notes so that in moments of lowness or confusion, you can remember the facts—you're capable, you're strong, and you can actually do this!

Do the Dang Dishes

If you're a Type 4, there is a good chance dishes are sitting in your sink right now. Or there's a pile of laundry in your corner that has been making its home there for the past few weeks. Maybe there are still some unpacked boxes in your new apartment. Maybe you're still living off microwavable food because that's what's working for you right now, and your internal world is so much more of a priority than making a proper meal. This may just be a hunch I have . . . but I think you sometimes struggle to take care of yourself as an Individualist. When you spend all day surrounded by conversations you can't get out of, when you have to wake yourself up at an ungodly hour, when the emotions you're processing keep you up past your normal bedtime or fuel unreasonable expectations of yourself, or when you can't get out of going to that party you previously committed to, the very life can get sucked out of you. It can feel like your dreams and drive to understand your authentic self and your real-life obligations that never seem to stop piling up have collided in a big crash. The condition of your apartment or office or kitchen can always wait when you'd rather ponder your dreams and the mysteries of life. But trust me, Individualists, take a leap of faith, and just vacuum. Wipe down the counters. Take out the trash. Clean out the fridge. Do the dishes in the heat of all of your thoughts and feelings. Because in the thick of those thoughts and feelings is when you need something real to ground you the most. Imagine diving into your bed with clean sheets after an emotionally exhausting day. Imagine eating a filling, nutritious meal while watching that new period drama. You are not incapable of this; you have to resist the urge to only feel or only think. You have to *do*. I promise, you'll feel so much better. You'll also find that your brain will have more space to think and process in the way you want. I give you permission to come tell me off if this fails.

Be Upset and Be Thankful

The harsh reality is that no matter how well we take care of ourselves, how hard we work, or how intentional we are, not only are we imperfect but so is the very fabric of our universe. We live in a broken world, where really sad things exist, and sometimes those sad things can happen to us or people we love and it's completely out of our control. Individualists feel this reality in the essence of their soul, and it affects them to some degree almost every day. Life will never be in your control and, honestly, Individualists, it's okay to be bothered by that. It's okay for that reality to be confusing and hard, because it is! You're allowed to sit with the realities of this life and be upset about them. But the more effort we put into sitting and reconciling all of the unknown, potential occurrences in our life, the more we miss opportunities to be completely thankful for our life as we're in it today. The cool thing about having human emotions is that we have the capacity to hold both sadness and gratitude—not just separately but together at the same time. We are wired to be upset, but we are also wired to be thankful. So, my sweet Individualist, as you experience worry or stress from the uncontrollable outcomes in life, feel it . . . process it . . . and say thank you for what you have. Say thank you for your healthy family, friends, and body. Say thank you for your job, your passions, your comfortableness. Build lasting memories and learn to be incredibly thankful for what is present in front of you. And then, keep going. Keep breathing and keep living.

What's Wrong with Ordinary?

Individualists live their lives in the pursuit of the unordinary. They often prefer what's dramatic and unconventional over everything else because it feels more expressive and relatable to them. The thought of being plain or ordinary makes them gag, and it's hard for them to take others who are ordinary or pursue the things that are "trendy" seriously. This snobbery, in a sense, can keep Individualists from experiencing the things they're actually afraid of missing out on. It can keep them from friends who might love them really well. My question for Individualists is: Since when are you not special if you're ordinary? Since when do you not matter if you're just like everybody else? Since when are you shallow because you like the song that's #1 on Spotify? Since when are you not unique anymore because someone else is also unique? Since when is "different" what makes you valuable? I think the real root of the issue for Individualists is that because they define their worth based on their originality, that's how they measure the worthiness of others as well. Individualists, I want to encourage you to start defining your worth based on things apart from your perceived originality. I want to encourage you to start seeing who someone is underneath their "ordinariness" or "trendiness." Maybe you were right about them, but maybe you were wrong. And maybe you were wrong about yourself, too.

Comparison Is What's Killing You

One of the healthiest things Individualists can do for themselves is spend an entire day away from their phone and off the internet. Why? Because, like many of us, Individualists can easily become disconnected from reality when they spend too much time using technology. Consistently unplugging can help to heal the root issue of Individualists' relationship with technology, as well as create more stability in their lives. What is the root of the relationship trouble, you ask? Comparison. All of us have dealt with the weight of it, but Individualists usually feel it more deeply, or are more connected to it, than the rest of us. They often don't see themselves in the people they're surrounded by in real life, and they definitely don't see themselves in the people they follow on social media. They may already feel misplaced and unsettled, but the comparison trap hidden in social media only makes them feel more isolated, flawed, and alone. The reason I titled this tip "Comparison Is What's Killing You" is because Individualists tend to personalize this cycle of the comparison trap, believing that it is specifically an issue with the essence of who they are. "Why can't I just scroll past posts without comparing myself like other people can?" you may ask yourself. As an Individualist, you should be proud that you can't scroll like the majority of us, because social media can be a harmful and hurtful place. You should be proud that you're aware of how damaging social media can be and how it is affecting you. Don't be ashamed of believing the best about people and wanting social media to be an authentic place. Start by squashing the comparison trap with a healthy routine like unplugging for periods of time—you may even then become empowered to try making social media the better place you believe it can be.

Just Do It

Just do the thing. You know, the book you want to write. The business you want to start. The painting or song you want to create. The album you want to make. The speech you want to give. The platform you want to establish or movement you want to start. The audition tape. The big, larger-than-life dream, the one that's so real and fulfilled in your mind. Just do it, sweet Individualist. It may not be everything you envisioned, but at least you did it. You may not get the answer or reaction you fantasized, but you did it. You may not like how it turns out, and it may not be perfect, but you did it. You may be thinking even now, *If it's not going to be what I have imagined, why even bother doing it?* And to that, I say: because you will have actually done it. It won't be just a dream anymore. It won't be something you just wished and longed for. It will be something you went for, fought for, and sweat for. It will be something you worked for, cried over, and overcame. The action of doing involves more than just what will happen in the end; it also involves the process of how we get there—the way it grows us, refines us, strengthens us. "Doing it" is about more than just accomplishing something. Sometimes you have to do it just to kick fear in the ass.

There's Life Out Here, Too

Sometimes I wish I could get inside an Individualist's brain. You may be thinking, *It's a dank, scary place*, but you might not know just how rosy and bright the world can look. Because Individualists often think of how beautiful things ought to be, they have a tendency to be disappointed by what already is beautiful. Individualists receive so much shame from others because of this, but before I give you some self-care advice in this area, I want you to know that your ability to not just believe the best but *visualize* the best in the deepest and most unconventional way is something to be admired. The world craves your imagination just as much as you do. Let us into your world! I know that it's stunning. I know there are so many well-written words and melodies, so many beautiful works of art inside your mind, which is why my challenge to you is to remember that there is life out here, outside your creative mind, too—and it can be just as beautiful because of what you bring to it. Because of what you shared with it, and with us. Because of the talent, gentleness, tenacity, and passion you can't but help to pour out. Pour it out here!

It's Not Only About How You Feel

I think it's important for every human to find a cause about which they're passionate, but the practice of finding this cause and fighting for it is essential to an Individualist's self-growth and self-care—because Individualists can easily get stuck in complacency and inaction and thinking solely about themselves. By doing things like taking up an important cause or volunteering in their community, however, Individualists can better see how even the smallest actions can impact others in a positive way—or maybe even change their life. They can better see that there is a whole world operating and revolving, and it's not revolving around them. When Individualists become face-to-face with injustice in the world, they can be a force of nature. The power of their belief that beauty is found in pain is something completely unique to who an Individualist is—this passion lies at the very core of their being. Serving others helps them unlock this passion in an unexpected way, and doing so consistently can really alter the perspective of an Individualist forever.

Let Things Be

One of the most endearing yet humorous messages I've ever received from an Individualist was about how she could make exercise more meaningful. This is a valid question because a lot of fitness and diet culture can feel meaningless or empty, but this specific Individualist proceeded to ask me how exercising can be more awakening, artistic, and self-expressive. She wanted to go deeper into her feelings and thoughts through the act of exercise, and then maybe if she was able to connect to that, she'd want to do it more. The main reason why this Individualist was frustrated with working out is because it seemed to take her *too much* out of her head. I gently explained in my response to her that I personally think exercising is important for Individualists because of how it can disconnect them from their heart and head. It forces them to take a half hour, give their brain a break, and connect with their body in a different, physical way. In a sense, one of the main purposes of exercising is to better connect yourself with your body so that you can proceed to think and feel more clearly, as opposed to retreating deeper into how you are already thinking and feeling. I tell this story because a healthy self-care practice for Individualists is to let things be what they're meant to be. Exercising may not be the most artistic experience, but what if it's not meant to be? What if the reason why it benefits you is because of how it opposes your nature? Individualists tend to read between the lines with every activity, human, or experience they encounter, when sometimes there is nothing hidden. Things just are the way they are. People are just who they're meant to be. Experiences are just experiences. And that's okay. Individualists need to realize that not everything in life has to have deep, personal meaning to them.

You're Not Just Unique

Individualists seek to distinguish themselves from the people around them—whether that's through their clothes, achievements, philosophies, or aesthetic. They want people to look at them and say, "Wow, she's different from everyone else." You won't catch many Individualists you know on an app, listening to a playlist, or doing something that most people think is cool. Individualists pride themselves on being unique because they feel so deeply different from others internally. They've never felt like they've "fit in" or "fit the mold" of the people around them—and they've learned to find confidence in this since they've felt insecurity around it for so long. I want to celebrate this confidence in Individualists because it truly is an amazing quality to possess, but I also want to challenge them in it—because when an Individualist doesn't feel unique anymore, they don't feel like life is worth living. They feel as though a very personal part of their identity has been stolen, and they revert to this lie that they will never be able to go about life the way other people do. Uniqueness sometimes feels like all Individualists have because they're so terrified of losing any sense of self. They want to have an identity. And they can even get to a point where they attack or tear down anyone who attempts to take that identity away from them. My question for Individualists in light of this is: What if you're not just unique? What if defining your worth in this one word, this one trait, is actually limiting who you are to begin with? What if you're also kind? Hardworking? Loyal? Valued? Loved? What if your value to others isn't that you're different or unique, but simply because you're you?

Let Us Understand

Individualists have spent most of their life feeling misunderstood, so much so that it's become a comfortable space in which they can live. In a sense, Individualists would rather still be misunderstood, because being understood means their life may be boring. What if when they're understood, the intoxicating, intense roller coaster inside their mind stops? What do they do then? What do they feel then? Being understood means letting themselves be loved for who they are—but that's extremely uncomfortable for Individualists. The more that people just don't get it, the more they can easily continue on as they are, without having to change. It's a complicated space to occupy—longing for what isn't, yet when it comes, you then long for what was. Being understood also chips away at their identity of being too complex and complicated for anyone to "get." Individualists base a lot of their identity in their individuality, so being understood could mean an Individualist has lost what has identified them their whole life. And then, who are they when they're finally seen and loved? When they're understood and heard? When they're accepted for what they believe makes them unacceptable? If you're an Individualist, I want to encourage you to let someone understand you, perhaps someone you've pushed away because they came too close to knowing exactly who you are. Let someone uncover you, and then let them seek to understand you—underneath the "unique" and "different," where they can see how sweet your soul is.

Pursue a Healthy Sleep Regimen

Most Individualists I know struggle with sleep. Individualists can be prone to all-encompassing anxious or sad thoughts, which can lead to insomnia. They can also completely lose their sense of time when they get caught up in things like thoughts, feelings, media, or music. They find their sleeping patterns heavily depend on their mood, which subsequently affects how they function every day. I want to encourage Individualists to do whatever it takes to improve their sleep by pursuing a healthy sleep regimen. I know routine may not sound appealing to you, but treating yourself to good sleep is more than just routine; it's about loving life a little bit more because you'll feel your best. You can still be creative, and eat or watch whatever you want, but begin to notice what times of the day you feel sleepy, when your body is naturally inclined to sleep, and when you are very much wired and awake. Become self-aware of your body—what is it saying to you? Intuitively listen to how it's communicating through energy levels and mood changes. I think a lot of Individualists experience cyclical sadness because they're not taking care of their bodies—they're hungry, sleepy, or tired—not just because they feel flawed. So do what you think will be best for your body, and then stick to it. Bring in an accountability partner. Start a blog about your journey. Whatever it is that will help you sleep better, even if that's going to the doctor to get everything checked out, fight for your sleep. It's worth it.

You Are Not What You Create

Individualists profoundly identify with what they create. Whether it's in the realm of the arts or science and systems, they view what they make for others as an extension of their soul. If that extension of who they are is not appreciated, respected, or seen accurately for its essence, Individualists tend to withdraw from the world until someone finally gets it. They develop this self-sabotaging pattern for two reasons. The first reason is that Individualists hate receiving harsh or overly critical feedback from others on their work. However, it's important for them to know that in order to continue to grow in whatever skill we possess, we have to let others see it and make suggestions. The best way to avoid unnecessary or unhelpful feedback, though it's not always possible, is to find a handful of creatives or mentors you respect—people you know want what's best for you and know what it will take to make your dreams come true—who can offer authentic, honest, and constructive criticism. The second reason why Individualists develop this self-sabotaging pattern is because they can believe they are only what they create. They've placed so much of their identity in, and poured so much of their heart and soul into, what they produce that when the work they are doing does not feel good enough, it can be detrimental to their self-esteem. It's deeply personal to them. That being said, I encourage Individualists to begin *de*personalizing what they create. You can start small, so rather than saying, "This is my painting," say, "This is a painting that I created." Although you still own what you made, it doesn't own you anymore. It's not attached to your soul's essence.

HOW TO TAKE CARE OF
THE TYPE 4 IN YOUR LIFE

Avoid Invalidating Language

If you have a Type 4 in your life, you know how much they value emotional honesty. They desire to connect with their authentic selves and the authentic selves of others, and this desire can exhaust them due to their innate drive to chase depth and meaning in everything. Individualists want to create as much meaning and purpose in their life as possible— they want to sustain a beautiful environment, they want more people and things to explore, and they want to make both people they know and people they don't thankful that someone as unique as them exists. We admire our wonderful Individualists for being so committed to creativity and empathy in a time where it feels as though everyone is striving for the opposite, and sometimes that can lead us to thinking that they enjoy being the "tortured souls." The truth is, while Individualists do love the drama and intensity they naturally possess, they're also stuck. They're stuck in reconciling stability and exploration. They're stuck in regrets from the past and idealizations for the future. They're stuck in longing for more, less, and different. Because of this, the most authentic way you can love your Individualist is by taking their emotions seriously. Reach out to them about their passions, hopes, and dreams. But also ask them what they've been wrestling with in their minds, what's been weighing on their hearts. Individualists want to feel sought after and safe with those they love. The more an Individualist can feel like their feelings and struggles are valid, the more they will feel empowered to overcome them.

Be the String to Their Balloon

When you think of a balloon, you also think of the string attached to the bottom of it. When you're holding the string, the balloon stays with you, stays in your sight, and stays steady. When you let go of the string, the balloon will float farther and farther away, until it's so far gone that you can't even see it anymore. This can happen in many friendships and relationships with an Individualist. Although they decidedly do *not* need someone to rescue them or change them, they do need someone who will come along and help keep them from withdrawing and retreating into their internal fantasies. Being the string to the balloon means listening to all of the amazing dreams that live inside the mind of an Individualist and, rather than telling them to go do something about them, sitting down and helping them do something about them. Help make sense of their thoughts, and break them down into easy, actionable steps. Being the string to the balloon means showing Individualists how much wonder can be found in the realities of life by helping to create those beautiful moments for and with them. Being the string to the balloon means being an open ear and a voice of reason, holding your sweet Individualist with less judgment and more empathy. Being the string to their balloon means encouraging deep discussions during practical activities, so things that have to get done (like the laundry or dishes) still do, but they've been made more purposeful and memorable through the conversation.

Bring Magic to Little Things

Individualists live for the small moments in life—the moments when they feel as though magic is sitting in a cozy chair and drinking their morning coffee during a quiet morning. Or the way the light hits the floor at 1:30 P.M. in a certain room in their house. Pay attention to the little things that Individualists love, and then remind them about how beautiful life is with them. Notice when the light hits the floor a little more delicately at work; take a picture and send it to them saying "thought of you." Anything you know that makes Individualists appreciate real life is important to bring into theirs daily, because they can lose that appreciation as quickly as they found it. Pursuing the magic in little things with them also helps you discover the little things you enjoy, and can then share with your Individualist friend or partner. It may seem odd, but this practice shows Individualists that you're in this with them. You're looking for light, magic, hope, and beauty with them. Knowing and seeing how an Individualist has made your life better and brighter is one of the highest forms of respect and love you can show them—because that's ultimately what they want: to make a difference. Especially in the lives of the people they love.

THE OBSERVER

ALERT, INSIGHTFUL, CURIOUS,
INNOVATIVE, INTROVERTED, PRIVATE

CORE DESIRES:

To be self-reliant, competent, and useful

CORE FEARS:

Being inept, dependent, incapable, and depleted

ULTIMATE MOTIVATIONS:

To be smart, to get to the bottom of things,
to protect themselves from the unknown

AFFIRMATION:

"My needs are not a problem."

Observers are usually labeled "the quiet ones." The stereotype is the friend in the corner of the room at the party, usually with their earbuds in and head down looking at their phone, or the friend who skips the party altogether to be in the comfort of their own space. They don't mind being alone with their thoughts; they actually prefer it, and although they feel things deeply, most people perceive them as being rather unemotional and detached.

You Might Be an Observer If . . .

* You only have a certain amount of social energy in the day, and once you reach it, you will not be able to function unless you recharge.
* You are, admittedly, a creature of habit.
* Even if you're not a book nerd, you have a love for unraveling mysteries and riddles and probably know a lot about seemingly random, niche subjects.
* Anything—literally anything—can fascinate you. You are a curious person by nature.
* You enjoy believing that you are the smartest person in the room. It brings you confidence.
* Sometimes you hide your true self behind talking about what you know because it feels much safer.
* You find it hard to execute your goals because you want to make sure you have all the information, equipment, and tools before you get started.
* You don't mind spending time by yourself. In fact,

sometimes you can end up isolating yourself from the world if you're not careful.

- You sometimes hoard your energy, time, and love from others out of fear of becoming depleted.

5W4

Leaning into their 4 wing, Type 5s are a little more romantic, adventurous, and consumed with beauty. They believe that everything is possible with a little imagination. More introverted than their 5W6 friends, they are visionaries who have a drive to understand the intricacies of both the heart and the universe. They crave mental stimulation, and they feel things much deeper than they might let you know. 5W4s have a mysterious air to them, and they have a tendency to unintentionally draw people in with their quiet, gentle demeanor and intellect. They're wonderful advice-givers and amazing people to have in your inner circle. Remind your 5W4 friend today that they are capable, and they have what it takes.

5W6

Probably a little more extroverted than their 5W4 counterparts, 5W6s are fixated on mental, physical, and relational security. Their minds are constantly racing with tasks, ideas, and hypotheses, and they feel a deep-seated sense of responsibility to their family, friends, and the organizations of which they are a part. These Type 5s are more likely to chime in with a perfectly timed witty remark, and they can be awkward in the most endearing way. They desperately want to stay on top of everything in their life, and they are more prone to people-pleasing. If you have a 5W6 in your life, remind them that they are doing just fine—that they're not behind and they are loved.

WHY TYPE 5S NEED SELF-CARE

Observers have a quiet resilience and desire for the undiscovered in life. They ultimately want to feel capable and competent above everything else, which can cause them to disappear from the world when they believe that they aren't enough or that they don't have enough to take on all aspects of life. This leads to a rabbit hole of overthinking and researching, causing them to spiral into a cycle of self-neglect and cynicism. We need the Observers to take care of themselves because who they are apart from what they know is valuable and needed. Their gentle nature and quick mind help us to innovate, explore, and improve our world for the better.

SELF-CARE PRACTICES FOR TYPE 5S

Learn to Grow, Not to Understand

As an Observer, you have an insatiable longing for information. All of the Type 5s I know have a thorough understanding of fields and patterns that have nothing to do with their everyday life or career path. If you're in marketing, or biochemistry, or photography, there's a chance your Observer friend knows everything about algorithms, living organisms, and camera lenses, even if they're an engineer. To live is to learn for Observers, and they wouldn't have it any other way. It's what they're comfortable with and it makes sense to them. But what many Observers don't realize is that they are simply studying to gain knowledge, not to grow from it. Because they want to get to the bottom of all the world's mysteries, they can sometimes forget to get to the bottom of the things that actually matter to them. They may know everything about Peru's economy, or how to hike fjords in Norway, and thoroughly understand how Earth's magnetic pull functions, but pursuing things that allow them to take action and grow as deep-hearted individuals can be difficult for them. If you're an Observer, remember that you are fully equipped and capable of handling whatever growth may bring. Yes, it is going to require energy. It probably will require some time. It may even require you to authentically connect with others in a way that feels depleting. But you can do it. You can take steps and feel tired and keep going. Keep learning, but learn to benefit and grow yourself, too. You're worth it.

Find Your Place

Observers struggle to be correctly understood by others. Their aloof, quiet nature—with bouts of sarcastic, intelligent humor—can be intimidating and confusing to a lot of the other Enneagram types. As a result, more extroverted types assume there's something wrong with Observers because of how quickly they can lose their energy in social settings. Type 5s genuinely become drained emotionally, physically, and mentally quicker than most Enneagram types. I see so many people who try to change Observers—make them be more outgoing, more affectionate, more of what they're not—which forces Type 5s to feel like they need to be different so that they can better fit into their environment. The core goal of using the Enneagram is to grow into your best, most authentic self; it should never be used as a tool for shaming one's natural way of being. You and your personality were created with purpose and for a purpose. There is no mistake in how you were made and you deserve to be loved for your truest self. Everyone deserves to find their place in the world, including Type 5s—because you are capable of showing up in the world and making an impact for the better. You are competent and resilient in the face of setbacks and challenges, and there are people out there who will see these incredible qualities in you and celebrate them! There are jobs that are meant for you—your wiring, your makeup, your biology. So find your place and find your people. Not only will you feel loved but you will feel refreshed in the permission to be yourself unapologetically.

Get Jiggy With It

As a Type 5, you may love or hate me for suggesting this depending on your level of introversion, but I think dancing is one of the most therapeutic activities a Type 5 can do. Why, you ask? Let me give you some stats. According to a study published in the journal *Neuroscience and Biobehavioral Reviews* in 2017 by Marko Punkanen, Suvi Saarikallio, Outi Leinonen, Anita Forsblom, Jeena Kulju, and Geoff Luck, dancing supports intellectual brain functions, boosts memory, and stimulates nerve growth factors. You read that right: dancing is *for* neuroplasticity. And I think it heals a Type 5 brain uniquely from other types (although there is no research to back that one up, sorry!). Based on the experiences of other Type 5s that I know, dancing is one of the few activities that can actually take their mind off all the things going on inside their head. Once they are able to get over the initial awkwardness of it, it's unbelievably freeing for them. So here is my challenge to you, Type 5: start by taking small, salsa steps. Turn up your favorite song, and then just have a dance party! If dancing with some of your best buds makes you feel more comfortable, throw an intentional dance party with them. Take your partner to a beginner dance class, or watch a YouTube dance tutorial. Find a dance style that works for you, whether it's salsa, hip-hop, contemporary, or maybe just flailing around in the security of your bedroom. Do your best to not overthink it. Just try it out!

Start the Project

When I was living in Dallas, I attended an "Enneagram in Relationships" group for five weeks. It was meant to create a space where participants could work through Suzanne Stabile's book *The Path Between Us* and also be equipped to lead the study ourselves one day with others. There were actually quite a few Observers in the class, all of whom were happy to speak up about their tendencies in this emotionally intelligent setting. During one of the sessions, we talked about how we accomplish and approach our goals based on our Enneagram type. The Observers in this particular class talked about how they tended to create in-depth, elaborate plans for a project but never really execute them. One Observer in particular talked about how she had been wanting to start a vegetable garden in her backyard. She bought all the right equipment, spent hours watching YouTube videos on the best gardening practices, and committed her free time to learning everything she could about nurturing vegetables with care. One day, she went outside into her backyard to measure the space where she wanted to build one of her planters, and realized that the parts for this planter had been sitting in her backyard for three months. This person never actually began the building process, even though she knew how to do it all in detail. All the soil, equipment, and seeds were in a pile, just waiting to be used. Ultimately, this person had spent so much time studying and preparing for the gardening process that she had missed the prime season to actually start gardening. Observers have a hard time trusting their qualifications, even if they are well-versed and experienced in a subject. So to all of my Type 5s out there, start the project. Start toward the goal. Start the renovation. You have everything you need within you. Don't miss out on seeing your dreams become a reality. You have what it takes.

Set and Know Your Limits

If you've ever had a friend who doesn't text or call or seemingly disappears from social media for a few days or even weeks without you realizing it, your friend might be a Type 5. Recharging is both a necessity and a habit for 5s. It is vital for their mental, spiritual, and physical health to spend time by themselves, and they are also completely comfortable with being alone for extended periods of time. Their comfort with being alone can be their greatest asset, but it can also be their enemy. The husband of one of my friends is a Type 5. I remember him talking one day about how if they could live in a tiny house deep in a forest or on a large plot of land, he would be content for the rest of his life. His wife, a Type 2, chimed in and said, "This is why we make such a good pair, though. I'm down to help him achieve this dream, but also be there to help him reconnect with others. Because he would literally forget to connect with society after that, whereas I would go insane without people for that long."

So, Type 5s, this is your friendly reminder that—even if you're lucky enough to have a Type 2 in your life—you need to know your limits and embrace them. Don't be ashamed of when you need to head home, take a break, or leave the group chat. That being said, set limits within your limits. Become aware of how much time your body, mind, and heart truly need to recover, and limit yourself to that allotted time. Don't overextend your alone time—rejoin the world and your relationships wholeheartedly. Share with others what you've discovered, and be bold about it. You will surprise yourself with how good you feel afterward.

Make Yourself Available

Observers, I know reading that statement made you cringe . . . so hear me out. What if your unique perspective and understanding of complex patterns helps put the puzzle pieces together for someone else? What if opening yourself up and sharing how you feel inadequate can help thousands of others see that they are not as alone as they feel? There's a powerhouse Type 5 poet you may have heard of named Morgan Harper Nichols, who began her journey as a self-employed artist by simply posting a piece about how inadequate she felt on Pinterest in 2016. What's crazy is that four years before this, I met Morgan in a songwriting class at a camp in Nashville. We were instructed by Morgan to go around the room and sing for her. When I tell you the only song I could remember in that moment was "Happy Birthday," I mean it. I froze. After my nerves settled down a bit, I ended up singing a very poorly written song that I wrote and stood out like a sore thumb. After the class, I introduced myself to Morgan, and it felt like meeting the queen, although I'm sure she didn't see herself in that way. She told me my song had beautiful imagery.

Eventually, she followed me on Instagram, and she engaged with every small business or movement I tried to create. And that's why I believe her poetry defied all algorithms and exploded across the internet. Because when Type 5s make themselves available, they can spark real and meaningful change. When she started to gain popularity on social media, her in-box began flooding with messages from men and women, just like me, who were begging her to keep sharing her writing. Morgan is consumed by the light and heavy stories of individuals around the globe, and we all watched as she made herself available to those messages, because we needed her. She is a rock on social media in the midst of a turbulent sea of disagreement and divisions, and, thankfully, she found her passion in this sea. Morgan continues to write poetry and raise a family, all while singing and sharing with strangers. So, to you, you beautiful Type 5: Feel empowered. See how Morgan is a vital piece in a big puzzle. See how you are similarly a vital piece in a big puzzle. See how your understanding of mystery can be a guide for a searching soul. We ask for your availability because we need you.

Nature Is the Best Companion

Nature does not beg for your attention and love, rather it beckons for your gaze and admiration. It calls you to be active, but active in silence. As a Type 5, sometimes connecting with your physical body can seem daunting. Lifting weights, running, and traditional exercise can feel like putting a square peg in a round hole—it just doesn't fit for you. As predominantly "thinking" people, 5s are constantly exercising their minds. Their natural time orientation is to the past, making it hard for them to connect to the present moment. They're running circles around systems.

Climbing up internal mountains. Doing mental preparation for their days and weeks ahead. When there is a lack of connection between this internal exercise and your physical exercise, it can start to make you feel trapped. Type 5s may even feel numb to their surroundings after long periods of physical stagnancy, which is why exercise is a necessary part of keeping not only your body healthy but also your mind. The more you consistently pursue exercise, the more mental clarity you will have. You will have more room for new thoughts and a greater ability to focus on the small things. So today, dear 5, I'm pushing you to find what feels good to you. You have permission to not exercise conventionally as long as you move your body in some way. Try spending your time to recharge hiking, skiing, surfing, climbing, walking, or simply enjoying what nature has to offer you. Doing this will benefit your health and your sanity.

Actually Treat Yourself

As a Type 5, you probably are a very minimalistic person. You know what you like, you know what you need to survive, and anything beyond that you believe to be impractical. Because of this, you tend to deny yourself things or experiences. There are probably a few coffee spots you've been wanting to try, or something that you've always wanted to get yourself that might even make your life more efficient, but you always convince yourself it isn't necessary. Type 5s secretly grew up believing that it's not okay for them to be comfortable in the world—whether that was because they always felt intruded upon by family members or nonverbal communication from others showed them that their inner needs don't actually matter. However this belief came about for you as a 5, it shows up more than you realize, and if no one has ever told you that you are allowed to feel comfortable in this world, let me tell you . . . you are allowed to feel comfortable in this world. You are allowed to feel taken care of and at ease. Your needs are important and they matter. Let this be your permission slip to get what you really want. Your wants are not a problem or an inconvenience. So get yourself that new backpack, or espresso machine, or planner . . . whatever it is! In the words of Tom Haverford and Donna Meagle: TREAT YO SELF!

Let Yourself Be Challenged

I believe in intuitions and inspirations.
I sometimes feel that I am right. I do not know that I am.
—Albert Einstein

Type 5s are some of the smartest people in the world. They are intellectuals by nature, and if you don't know this by now, mental stimulation, whether in a classroom or on Reddit, thoroughly brings them joy. Think of the 5s as mini Albert Einsteins. One of my Type 5 friends, who had been reading a biography of Einstein's life, once said he felt an unexplainable connection to the way Einstein felt a constant inner curiosity. Every human, but especially every 5, truly has the capability of being a genius in their field of choice, but it comes with one cost: being open to being challenged. Type 5s desire to be capable and competent above all else, so feeling that they are the smartest in the room admittedly also brings them joy. When they feel outsmarted, the humiliation that follows can send them into a tailspin of isolation and never-ending research. Asking questions in the heat of the moment can seem draining to them, when curling back up into their minds to sort it all out is way more comfortable. In the system of the Enneagram, every number begins to integrate with another number on the Enneagram when they exhibit growth. For Type 5s, their growth number is 8, "The Challenger." Type 8s are self-assured, tenacious, and quick to give their opinions. They have this gut intuition that makes sharing and asserting their capabilities second nature, and 5s have the capacity to do this, too. Type 8s love to debate for the heck of it, and 5s are the most "qualified" to debate with others because of how much they know. So, as a 5, don't be afraid to jump in and open yourself up to the unknown of a debate in the name of learning! I can guarantee you will surprise yourself with your own self-assurance.

Say "Yes"

Type 5s have this admirable gift of knowing when to say "no." They know their limits. They have a keen awareness of what they can't handle—and they set strong boundaries they don't often cross. The unfortunate flaw in this amazing quality is that while 5s know very well what they can't handle, they do not credit themselves for what they *can* handle. They tend to store up a reservoir of energy that they may or may not use, because they never know when they will need to draw upon it in times of emergency. This happens especially within their relationships. The issue is, there often are no emergencies or crises they have to deal with, but they still convince themselves to keep this energy locked away, just in case. So as 5s receive invitations and opportunities for themselves to connect or move up in their career, they often start to believe this narrative: *I do not have enough internal resources to handle all that life is offering me.* But in the spirit of letting yourself be challenged by others, I have to disagree with 5s on this one. Every Type 5 I know has shown unmatched resilience and dedication to what they believe in without even realizing it. One of my closest friends is a 5, and she once worked onsite at a safe house with women who wanted to change their life in the wake of homelessness and human trafficking. She led family dinners, led studies in spiritual and functional skills, and listened to heavy, emotional conversations with women taking huge steps toward healing. Would she tell you that this drained her? Yes, she would. But would she tell you that she was proud of herself for jumping into it? Yes, she would. Would she also tell you that she decided to leave that job to pursue her actual passion in life? Yes, she would. Type 5s, give yourself credit. You are great at discerning what is good for your life. You can do more than you think, and there is a plan for your life that is larger and grander than you could've ever thought up or imagined for yourself. So say yes. Say yes when it's scary. Say yes when you don't feel as though you are enough. Say yes to making yourself available to personal, relational, and vocational growth.

Discover Your Inner Lion

Every Type 5 holds a remarkable power within them. From a young age, Type 5s learned how to defy the odds in some sense. They learned that things in life can be unjust, and a profound fire began burning in them for something more, something better. But somewhere along the way on their journey of growing up, this fire was dampened by the same things that lit the spark. Fearing uselessness and incapability, the injustice of this world began to overwhelm and exhaust Observers. However, Type 5s still have this fire secretly burning in them, whether they've realized it or not. In fact, it's a blazing, all-consuming fire. But it's locked away and hidden, like a lion in a zoo cage. Observers have tamed and trained this intensity to stay in its place in order to survive their environment, at the cost of leaving behind what was once wild and mighty. My biggest challenge to every Type 5 who happens to read this book is to rediscover your inner lion. Recall the rhythms and melodies of its roar. When you've done that and start to feel this fire within you burn once again, let the lion out of its cage. Return it to the wild, return it to its passions, and most of all, let its roar be heard by all.

Create and Complete
Small, Reachable Goals

My good Type 5 friend Kristen is wired to assist. What I mean by this is that she is gifted in keeping things organized, in putting together what seems impossible, and seeing all of the little steps that need to happen in order to get the big picture. Type 5s are amazing at doing this with other people, but I've found that they are not as great at doing this for themselves. They are often intimidated by their giant visions and fantasies and can get stuck in the continual breaking down of the big picture. Getting out of this rut requires you to step outside yourself for a minute, as though you are looking at these goals like they were someone else's. Give yourself the advice you would give others and create a brief list of things you can do today to get you where you want to go. Try not to let the list exceed three to five things. Focus on creating reachable and attainable goals. You've got this!

See That You're Doing Just Fine

A lot of the 5s I have talked to in my work with the Enneagram often talk about how they have a hard time remembering that they are actually doing okay. Observers *despise* feeling behind or scattered. The funny thing is that most of the time they aren't behind on things at all. They are often mentally ahead of the rest of us and can forget to recognize how well they're doing. So, Observers, I'm going to give you an exercise. Take out a journal and write about who you were, what you were doing, and what was going on this time last year. Go with your gut. Be honest with yourself. After you've done that, take a second to think about who you are now, what you are running after, and what your daily life is like currently. I'd say for the majority of 5s reading this, you're going to see that you've truly made progress. You took steps, big and small, that have developed something new in you. Look back and see that you're doing just fine. Look around and see that everything is okay. Look ahead and see that there are far better things coming.

Believe You Are Not a Burden

It breaks my heart that so many 5s in this world believe they are a burden to others—that their voice will inconvenience, that their needs will interrupt. Type 5s are limited in their sight in this way, because the truth is, we want to be interrupted by them. Almost every person who has an Observer in their life is beckoning for their thoughts, feelings, and ideas to come to the surface—because the Observers' insights are so wholeheartedly and genuinely wanted by those that love them. Taking care of someone you love and feeling trusted by them is one of the most amazing experiences you can have in this life, but 5s feel disqualified from this.

They don't want to feel this way; it's just what they grew up believing about themselves. I'm sure that somewhere along the way, someone or something communicated to you that you were, indeed, a burden. And as angry as that makes you feel, this is a huge part of the Type 5's growing process. Because what if, my lovely Type 5, you are not a burden, no matter what someone else communicates? What if the things other people project onto you don't deflect from or chip away at the value of your being? You are never a burden. And you have to believe that about yourself first.

HOW TO TAKE CARE OF
THE TYPE 5 IN YOUR LIFE

Actually Respect Their Space

If you have a Type 5 in your life, you know that they love their space. Home provides a safe haven for them, more so than for most of the types, and they genuinely look forward to having time to withdraw into themselves. Rather than trying to change this about them, learn how to lean into it with them. This is the Observer's way of recharging, and affirming it with your words and actions will mean a great deal to them. Give Type 5s the permission to leave you to read, or replenish their mental energy in complete silence if they need to. If you show this level of respect for their process, they will show this level of respect for yours. Take the extra time to discover what it means for *you* to recharge, and use the hour or two that they take for themselves and use it for yourself, too. They will be so thankful for your consideration, and they will also be proud to see you taking care of yourself and your needs without relying on them to do so. Doing this develops a deep level of trust between you and the Type 5 in your life, and it takes a huge, unspoken weight off their shoulders. Type 5s desire to be there for you in your deepest need, but they also desire to see you be as self-sufficient as they are.

Learn About What They Love with Them

Chances are, the Type 5 in your life is obsessing over something right now. Whether that's space, marketing, Esportz, brain chemistry, or gardening, the possibilities for a Type 5 to learn are endless. And whatever they are into right now, they will not rest until they figure out the depths of it. Type 5s are incredible teachers, and they desire to see others learn just as much as they seek to learn. So if you are friends with a Type 5, or are in a relationship with one, take some time to understand what they're obsessed about today. Ask them to teach you what they're learning, or do your own research and ask them what they think about it. Observers will always require intellectual stimulation of some kind, and they will feel incredibly loved when you hash out the mysteries of the universe with them.

Empower Them to Show Up

Lastly, as you learned from this chapter, Type 5s can sometimes subject themselves to timidity due to their core fears. When they fear the possibility of incompetence, they isolate themselves to disengage with the weight that they feel. While sometimes Type 5s need to be freed from these obligations, there are other times when it is necessary and good to stand tall in the thick of them. In those times, help your 5 see how they are *wanted* as opposed to needed. Release the pressure of performance and focus on your desire to simply be with them in the midst of these circumstances. Even if they get annoyed with you at first, keep empowering them to show up. When things at work are piling on, when friendships are beckoning for attention, when their partner is requiring delicate love, remind them that they are indeed capable of taking everything on with power and courage.

TYPE 6

THE LOYALIST

RELIABLE, APPROACHABLE,
DETERMINED, ENGAGING, TRUSTWORTHY

CORE DESIRES:

To have support, guidance, and belonging

CORE FEARS:

Being unprepared, unstable, or without reassurance

ULTIMATE MOTIVATIONS:

To attain hope and truth, to be certain,
to understand their trustworthiness and that of
others, to find validation and security, to belong
to something bigger than themselves

AFFIRMATION:

"It's okay to trust myself."

Enneagram Type 6s, also known as "Loyalists," are often referred to as the "glue" of our families, organizations, and society. They are the friends that are prepared for every scenario and they are usually more concerned with physical safety and security than everyone else. They are also natural-born team players and are the most concerned for the common good than any other Enneagram type. Type 6s truly desire to see their loved ones be successful, even at the price of their own success and well-being. Loyal to a fault, once you have gained the trust of a Type 6, they will fight for you and with you until the end.

You Might Be a Type 6 If . . .

- You find yourself very worried about the deterioration of your and your loved ones' physical health.
- You have talked yourself out of doing something due to a negative scenario that might happen if you pursued it.
- You have a serious rebellious streak that can show up at any time despite being a steadfast person. You love and hate the thrill of conquering your fears.
- You have strong bonds within your friend group, and you tend to enjoy dance parties, dressing up in fun costumes, and holding on to sentimental objects more than most people.
- You sometimes play devil's advocate in situations that feel uneasy to you, not to be defiant, but because you want to make sure the outcome is going to be okay for you and everyone else.

- You're *very* bothered by change. It can take you longer to adjust to new circumstances because unknowns are hard for you to cope with.
- You have a unique sense of humor and an unmatchable wit that others genuinely appreciate.
- You tend to ask many friends and family members what they think about big decisions because you have a very hard time trusting yourself.

6W5

With a 5 wing, these 6s tend to be more introverted and observant, preferring to stay behind the scenes than be in the limelight. Attention, even if it's earned, can make them feel uncomfortable, because deep down they believe a secret lie that they aren't actually capable of being in the position they are in. All 6s are secret keepers, but 6W5s will literally take your secret to the grave. They are tremendously trustworthy and loyal. They are skeptical, but in a genuinely curious way, and these 6s crave learning like they crave belonging. More likely to have only a few close friends, once these 6s open up to you, they are a complete and utter goofy delight. If you have a 6W5 in your life, give them a big hug, respect their space, and empower them to keep pursuing what they believe in!

6W7

Leaning into their 7 wing, 6s tend to be more bold and extroverted, but their inner turmoil is also a little more confusing than that of their 6W5 counterparts. With a 7 wing, 6s are constantly fighting between stability and adventure. They can get serious FOMO, and want to experience all the pleasures and delicacies of life, but they also desire to have complete stability and security. With this inner conflict, they can show up in the world more impulsively and can be much more unpredictable than the traditional 6 type. These 6s are also prone to having more acquaintances than 6W5s, as they tend to be more openly playful and welcoming. If you have a 6W7 in your life, rub their shoulders every now and then and remind them that they are indeed doing enough and are not missing out on the life that is meant for them.

WHY TYPE 6S NEED SELF-CARE

Type 6s are decidedly responsible, and they desire what will keep them safe in this life. More than anything, they want to feel like they belong in their environment, but this Loyalist tendency can cause them to stay in jobs, relationships, friendships, and situations that are not actually good for them in the long run. Being separated from their security can lead to an overwhelming fear of the worst-case scenario, causing them to spiral into pessimism. We need Type 6s to take care of themselves because who they are apart from what they provide is valuable and needed. Their warmth and reliability gives us courage and helps us to stick together through thick and thin.

SELF-CARE PRACTICES FOR TYPE 6S

When in Doubt, Box It Out

Most 6s probably already have some sort of wellness or workout routine, but there may be some anxiety tied to exercising because of how much they fear the physical and medical unknowns in their life. For 6s, working out can become more of a way to fight potential diseases than something that is fun, engaging, and used to boost endorphins. So if you're a Type 6, I challenge you to switch up your wellness routine. There's a warm-natured Type 6 I know who, at only five foot one, seems to be rather unassuming—until you put her in a boxing ring, that is. All the doubt she has in her mind about her job, her health, and her capability is completely silenced for the forty-five minutes she throws punches while training. She literally fights through her mental and physical roadblocks and has developed a confidence that takes root in place of where her doubt was planted. I think it's unreasonable for any human, but especially a Type 6, to expect to fully get rid of any sort of nervousness when it's within their nature. But you can choose whether you water the doubts and let them grow—or let them wither by watering your inner confidence and courage instead. Boxing can be a tangible way to step out of your head and take your insecurities into the ring. To be honest, they don't stand a chance against you, friend.

Think More Productively

Type 6s have no problem thinking through potential scenarios. In fact, when they let their mind wander, their imagination becomes a vivid reel of all the positive and negative things that have a chance of happening—not only on that particular day but throughout their entire life. One of the core fears Type 6s have is being unprepared for something that they need to handle. They are continually bracing their mind, heart, and body for the most challenging outcome in order to survive the worst scenario. Since Type 6s have a plan A, plan B, plan C, plan D, etc., it makes them incredible troubleshooters. As helpful as this quality can be, it can also be our sweet 6's greatest enemy. This drive for preparedness can lead them to have anxiety about everything and everyone in their life. As a solution, I encourage 6s to try exercises in productive thinking. This may mean running through the worst-case scenario in your mind, sitting with the most heart-wrenching outcome, and looking it dead in the face. You may just find you will come out of the scenario okay. You will find another job. You will meet somebody new. You will grow and walk through things with bravery, and you will see the other side.

Read Something Boring

You might have laughed at this one, or even rolled your eyes, but hear me out!

Type 6s tend to get stuck in states of overdrive. When they are stressed, they can become competitive and paranoid that someone is behind them about to steal everything they have worked toward. They can become extremely worried about where they stand in their organizations, teams, and friend groups, and the stress can build up in their physical body. Their thoughts swirl into tornados that can overtake them, and turning this stress off can feel like an impossible feat. During one of my counseling sessions, when I personally was in a season where I was struggling with terrible insomnia, my therapist gave me a suggestion that changed the game for me: read something boring. Think of a subject in high school or college that literally made you yawn with disinterest. Pick a good book or audio book that contains words or concepts you don't understand—perhaps it's a novel you could never get invested in—and then keep it on your nightstand. Every night at your bedtime, or even in the middle of the day if you desperately need a nap, read for as long as you can. I promise you will find yourself getting tired very quickly, and the process will slowly begin to ease your mind from going into overdrive.

Laugh Really, Really Hard . . . but Not Always at Yourself

Loyalists are very sarcastic individuals. They have a genuine, pure goofiness about them and are usually admired by others for their timely wit. But when Loyalists are under stress, they can take on qualities of a Type 3, also known as an "Achiever." In general, they can become competitive and jealous, easily embarrassed when they feel ill equipped and unqualified, and can lose their sense of humor and replace it with image-consciousness. Although in these kinds of situations, Type 6s ironically have a tendency to use self-deprecating jokes as a way to cover up their anxiety. They're still Loyalists, y'know! They will usually make fun of themselves in order to elicit laughter rather than criticism. In a way, this can be a healthy habit. Obviously, none of us should take ourselves so seriously that we can't laugh at our shortcomings and cringey moments. Type 6s, though, can sometimes take self-deprecation too far. After a while, they might end up playing the role of the "punch line," which can ultimately take a toll on their self-esteem. Loyalists overcompensate for the things they are worried about being seen as; at the end of the day, they just want to know that they're pleasing others with their work and are making the people they care about happy, even if it's at the cost of their pride. So as a Loyalist, seek to find balance. Continue to show up with snarky, playful remarks. Keep laughing, doing funny voices, and making impressions. Sometimes, yes, allow others to laugh with you in moments of clumsiness or uneasiness. But know your worth. Learn to recognize when you or others crossed a line and set boundaries. Your inherent worth and value to this world is not a laughing matter. Show this respect for yourself even if you're panicked. You deserve to be your biggest cheerleader.

Know That You Can Do Things

My amazing mom is a Loyalist. As a child, she was my biggest advocate, my greatest friend, and my anchor when things got difficult. She was never scared to speak the truth, and she showed so much courage in her boldness and in her beliefs. She tackled most things with cautiousness, while somehow maintaining a sense of fun and spontaneity. The countless road trips, the car ride sing-alongs, the midweek trips to Bath and Body Works or the mall . . . she was and still is my buddy. A lot of my favorite moments together involved driving to one of my many extracurricular activities or classes (shout-out to the moms and dads who have increased their car mileage by 100,000 by getting us to where we need to go). During one of these drives, she told me about a moment she had in college that ended up shifting her life pretty drastically. Before she attended cosmetology school, she was taking psychology and law classes. She wasn't sure if she wanted to become a psychologist or a lawyer, but she was trying out both options. One day before class, she shut off her car, sat in the parking lot, and stared at the scholarly brick building in front of her. She told me that in that moment, she was so overcome with fear that she couldn't even bring herself to go inside. She was fearful of being terrible at both practices, but also of being successful at them. She was so paralyzed by the possibilities that before she knew it, she had spent two hours in the car trying to decide if she could go in or not. She missed both of her classes, and eventually dropped out and pursued a new career

path. Even though she was thankful she found cosmetology and mod-
eling, she told me that, looking back at that moment, there was so much
her younger self didn't actually see. She was blinded by so much worry
that she couldn't see how well she was actually doing. She couldn't see
how much her classmates liked her. She couldn't see her passion for the
material she was learning. Looking back, she not only wished she had
given herself more credit but also that she would've seen how strong and
smart she was. "I made a great cosmetologist," she told me. "But I also
would have made an amazing counselor or lawyer. And at the end of the
day, the anxiety from the choices I had to make is what drove me to assume the worst about myself. My work ethic. My abilities." I know many
Loyalists have gone through what my mom experienced as well, and I
want to encourage you with her own words: Assume the best about yourself and about other people. In moments of doubt, choose to believe that
things are going to be okay and will work out either way.

Be Okay with "New"

Many Loyalists are traditionalists. This doesn't mean that Loyalists are
necessarily conservative or conventional, but they like to stay within the
lines most of the time. What I mean is if Type 6s are used to doing a certain
activity on Easter, Christmas, Thanksgiving, or any holiday, then *nothing*
is going to stop them from doing it every single year. When others do not
want to uphold their traditions, Loyalists can become defensive and offended. Moreover, they can often hold on so tightly to their traditions and
customs that they can lose sight of what their family or friends actually
want. This mindset can be hard for a Type 6 to change because they've
become reliant on the familiarity of it all. Loyalists find rest, safety, and

beauty in what they can expect every year. But do not misinterpret their dedication to tradition as sheer stubbornness—because they're fighting for something they really believe in and trust. That being said, Loyalists can sometimes miss out on the opportunity to build new traditions, or add a unique twist to what they've been doing for years. So my encouragement for a Loyalist who is struggling to let go would be to try changing your perspective! Do you actually enjoy running the Turkey Trot every year? Do you actually enjoy dyeing eggs every Easter? If yes, then great! But think of how many more traditions you could introduce to your family and pass down from generation to generation. How can you inspire your siblings, children, or parents to try something new? Because what if "new" isn't as detrimental as you think? "New" could be your new favorite holiday tradition. Keep an open mind. And if you know a Type 6 who is struggling with the newness, don't make them feel guilty about it. Understand that keeping a relatively open mind is scary for them, so reassure them and verbally praise their humility.

Let Your Gut Be Your New Guide

How to make the right decisions in life is a question that keeps Loyalists up at night. They don't want to jeopardize their security. They don't want to disappoint anyone. They don't want to make the wrong move. They would rather keep things the way they are than risk losing what is safe and familiar in their life. When Loyalists are faced with a decision, big or small, they have a tendency to consult a committee of people they've created. The sole requirement to be on this committee? Be able to give your opinion about what Type 6s should do. Loyalists will ask anyone, even if they're not a close friend or loved one, for their feedback on what choice they should make. After they've received this information from multiple parties, there are two possible outcomes: they take the time to analyze the information they received and end up doing what they wanted to do in the first place, or they allow everyone else to make the decision for them—even if it's not what they actually want. What Loyalists don't realize is that they have a strong gut; they make decisions internally without even noticing they're the ones actually making the moves, and they do this because they don't trust themselves. One of the best ways you can grow as a Loyalist is to set better requirements for who is on your committee, or as Brené Brown would call it, "your audience." Who are the people who would be in the front row, cheering you on, seeking what is actually best for you in life, whether or not it's what you want to hear? People who want to see you succeed, and who are just as loyal to you as you are to them? These are the only individuals who should be on your committee. Try to narrow it down to two or three people. Once you do that, you'll have a lot less conflict and background noise within your decision-making. You'll also realize that you can actually make good decisions on your own, and that there are people out there who want the best for you in life. As a helpful exercise, make a list of people who you think should be on your committee, and refer to it often. Then affirm that you can make good decisions on your own. Only allow the "front row" people to stand by you along the way. Being guided by others is important, yes. You learn from mentors and people who are older and wiser than you are. But let your gut be your guide, too. You know more than you think. Celebrate the wins! Recognize when you made not only a "good" decision but a decision faster than you normally would. It's worth celebrating!

Create a Vision Board

An often undiscussed trait of Loyalists is how they are generally hopeful about the future. This hope and optimism is often met with their inner committee's questions and voices, but hope still exists within them, and it runs deep. A way that you as a Loyalist can dig up this hope and keep it front of mind is by creating a vision board—whether it's by going the digital route and downloading pictures off Pinterest, Unsplash, or Tumblr, or by doing things the old-fashioned way and exploring your local Half Price Books and Goodwill for vintage magazines full of inspirational pictures. The way you do it is what should be best for you and your lifestyle. Once you've found your images, grab a bulletin board, arrange the photos individually, and then start pinning them up. Or if you're handy with Illustrator or Canva, create the collage digitally, and then print out the final product. Hang this up on your wall or in a place where you will see it every day. You can even create multiple vision boards—one for your room, one for work, one for your friends. Observe the photos and quotes you chose daily. Show yourself that the past, present, and future are worth getting excited about. It's okay to wear rose-colored glasses sometimes—because life can be rosy; it can be what you dreamed it to be. Keep creating, keep hoping, keep believing that the best is yet to come, and that it can also be found here and now.

Love Yourself as Much as
Your Pet Loves You

There is nothing better than the feeling you have when your pet looks up at you with so much love in their eyes, and anyone who says that animals don't feel that same connection with us is lying. I refuse to believe otherwise—especially when I think about all of the sweet glances (as well as all of the sassy ones) my childhood dog gave me when I was growing up. If you've ever had a pet, you not only know that there is an undeniable sense of loyalty you feel toward them but also that they feel this same sense of loyalty toward you. Even on days when you accidentally step on their paw or get frustrated with them, they still curl up with you at the end of the night. You always make up, and they never stop looking at you with that innocent admiration—because you're their primary source of guidance. Everything—their food, their toys, their rubs, their walks—is initiated by you. And they not only need you but also love you. It's unconditional. Loyalists are the same way. They're always fighting and fending for their people. Always looking out for those they love, always looking to them for guidance. Sometimes they receive love and affection back; other times they don't. But they always remain true. That being said, I want to challenge Loyalists to take that treatment of others and redirect it toward themselves. Show yourself the same love and respect that you would show to a friend, or that your pet would show to you. It's a rather odd analogy, but give yourself grace. Give yourself the same love you're continually giving others. Be loyal to who you are. Be loyal to loving your-self unconditionally.

S.T.O.P.

Depending on what kind of Loyalist you are, you respond to authority in one of two different ways. You can either be extremely submissive to the beliefs of people or theories that you believe are "higher" than you, or you can rebel against or be distrusting of anything that appears to be "authoritative." Some Loyalists can swing either way depending on the circumstance and the people involved, but Type 6s generally put either a lot of weight or no weight at all in the developed opinions and expectations of others. This almost resembles a war that they face within themselves on a daily basis: to trust themselves, or to trust someone else. To go with their gut, or check with one more human to see what they think. Loyalists have a constant inner committee of voices in their mind, not only working through the potential scenarios but also in a sense telling the Loyalist what to do. That they have to be loyal, that they have to move on; that they're not giving something enough time, that they've given it plenty of time already. This inner committee can become so loud it's overwhelming. Loyalists feel like they *have* to consult someone else for clarity. Or sometimes, these voices can become so overbearing that Loyalists start acting unpredictably. They'll take a tremendous risk or go somewhere or do something reckless just to get their mind to rest. These responses to their inner committee can be healthy in certain aspects. Asking one or two deeply trusted friends or family members can help Loyalists move forward and see the reality a bit clearer. Going with what you know to be true and jumping into something you believe in can show you that you are more capable than you thought to begin with. But my main tip for restless Loyalists who find themselves stuck in this inner battle is to simply slow down. Then take a breath. Inhale through your nose, exhale through your mouth. Open yourself to the voices in your mind. Rather than shutting them up or numbing out from them, listen to what they're saying. Become aware of the emotions you feel as you evaluate your thoughts. Next, I want you to give yourself permission. Permission to be confused, permission to need certainty or security . . . but then give yourself permission to trust yourself: who you are, or what your logic, your gut, your heart tells you—these are all bigger than the stress you are feeling at that moment. Your worries are not larger than you are; you will find yourself towering over them. After you've gone through these steps, proceed and pursue the outcome or plan you have put in place in that moment—whether that's to keep going about your normal day, to let things go, to just make a decision, or to talk to a few close confidants. You are allowed to be restless and bold at the same time. You are allowed to be confused, yet confident. Pursuing peace and going with the flow takes mindfulness and building up trust within yourself. Everything you are feeling is okay. Accept and then keep going.

Pursue Peace, Part I

Since Loyalists are usually stereotyped as anxiety-ridden people, they often aren't given a chance to explore a unique part of their integration of growth toward Type 9, the Peacemaker. When Loyalists grow into more Peacemaker tendencies, they become more easygoing and rested. If you are a follower/practitioner/lover of the Enneagram, you may know that each type tends to take on the traits of another type in times of stress.

For example, when Type 6s are developing confidence, and are generally feeling good about most things in life, they begin to feel more at peace with whatever they are facing. They aren't as easily set off by things they can't control, and they choose to be thankful for what they have, rather than working to protect their stability all the time. When in growth, Loyalists see that true stability and security comes from within. Practicing that inner steadiness takes work, and one small way Loyalists can begin to establish this within themselves is to pursue an atmosphere of peace. Although environmental peace only scratches the surface, I have found it makes a major difference in my life. My suggestion for you Loyalists is to grab a notebook and a pen, or just use the Notes app in your phone, and make a list of the smells, sensations, sounds, places, and objects that make you feel serene—whether that's the scent of your favorite candle or when your favorite meal is being made. How your skin feels after a bath or when you apply aloe lotion. When you hear the crashing of ocean waves and you open your eyes to see the crystal waters. Or maybe it's a vase filled with fresh lavender or eucalyptus. Go all out, be specific, and daydream about the things that make you feel warm inside. Once you've created this list, choose three of these things you can begin to incorporate into your everyday routine. Find pockets of time before breakfast or after dinner, whatever works within your schedule, and begin to fight for the peaceful things in your life. Let yourself look around and see things that remind you that you're okay and safe. Grab hold of the coziness of life, and let it deeply affect you. When you hold these blessings with thankful hands, and you learn to appreciate them every day, you're actually teaching yourself to only pay attention to the things that you can actually control.

Pursue Peace, Part II

Although you can control your environment, learning to focus on your thoughts—not letting them wander and escape—takes a lot of skill. Mindfulness is one of the hardest things to practice, and it is not for the faint of heart. It will get easier, but at first, your mind may become mentally exhausted from trying it. After I graduated high school, I worked at a camp for five weeks. This camp was meant to grow you physically, spiritually, and emotionally in ways you had never thought possible. And it definitely delivered on that promise. Every week, in preparation for a check-in with my counselors and the head of camp, the other counselors and I had to memorize a passage of Scripture to recite before our superiors. While studying Scripture one day, I came across a verse that resonated deeply with me. I had recently started seeing a side of myself that wasn't pretty. When you're in a place where all you have to entertain yourself with is your own thoughts, you tend to become quick to judge the people around you—those you know and those you don't really know at all. When I first started my job at the camp, I was quick to assume, rather than being quick to love. But one day, I took a passage of Scripture to heart, and I decided to practice mindfulness in a way I never had before. Every time I had a thought that was judgmental or encouraged me to make assumptions, I immediately recited the Scripture in my head. It was one of the most mentally and spiritually exhausting days of my life, because I was so presently aware of the thought patterns that had taken over my mind for so long. It was grueling to fight for something that did not come naturally to me, but I hoped that it would be worth it. After dinner that day, when we were cleaning up some of the chairs, a girl in my counselor group came up to me and said, "Christina, I just have to say, your positive attitude today was contagious. Not that you normally aren't positive, but you really showed so much care with every task you did. I felt really loved by you today, and I just wanted to tell you that!" Confused, grateful, and teary-eyed, I thanked her. The point of me telling this story is that this was the moment when I realized pursuing virtues such as peace, kindness, love, forgiveness, and self-control is an active, present fight. Fighting for mindfulness, and for what does not come naturally to you mentally, will always take consistent effort. If you don't feel peaceful after the first few times you try to replace negative or worrisome thoughts, I want you to know *that's normal and okay*. It's not a say-a-prayer, change-a-thought, and snap-your-fingers kind of deal. Pursuing peace is a process. And I want to empower you to fight for it. Freedom and courage is always within your grasp; it takes developing awareness while practicing mindfulness to recognize it. Fight for it. Even if you mess up on some days, don't give up. It won't be a perfect fight, but it'll be a worthwhile one.

Choose Gratitude

You know those moments in life that feel really amazing? There's a moment on that one Saturday in May when you get up early to go to the farmers' market, you see a few of your favorite people, you order a honey lemonade from your local coffee shop, and you look around and realize: life is really great right now. Not just because of this moment but also the moments outside it. You and your siblings are getting along, there's no drama between you and your friends or family, you've been killing it at work, you've even started working on a side project that you finally feel confident enough to pursue. I can picture you right now, sitting on a bench with your honey lemonade, smiling so big. But I can also see your smile slowly start to fade. I know what you're thinking: "What is going to come along and ruin this?" You begin to think of all the possible things that could happen and ruin what you have in this moment, and you become paralyzed. How can you prevent them and protect this happiness at all costs? Loyalists often opt to be realistic about things. Other Enneagram types may view this train of thought as being cynical or pessimistic, which, if the Type 6 isn't careful, can very well lead to that. But most of the time, Loyalists crash their own parade because they don't want to get hurt. They see their thought process as being sensible; not getting too excited or hopeful, playing devil's advocate, because who knows if this happiness or joy is real. Should they even be feeling joy with all of the horrible things that hang in the balance? My answer is yes! Let's rewind. Go back to the bench, the honey lemonade, and the big smile. As the thoughts of what could be spoiled begin to enter your mind, acknowledge them. Acknowledge that the thought or possibility exists. But don't entertain it any further. Rather, take this acknowledged thought and say thank you for what you have. You can say thank you to your family or friends, but I'm really suggesting to say a thank you to the universe, or whatever it is that you personally believe in. Practice gratitude for what you have. Because, say, down the road, if what you have is lost or spoiled, life will still go on; we can't control it. So wouldn't you want to recall these small moments in which you realized how blessed you are, and know that you savored them with gratitude? Worries, doubts, and suspicions don't stand a chance against thankfulness. It is your greatest weapon.

Enjoy Your Life to the Fullest

There is something so beautiful, yet so terrifying, about the thought of enjoying life—of not waiting to take that trip you have been dreaming of, but just going for it. Of choosing to be a little reckless and wild every once in a while. Of not studying that extra hour. Of not working that Saturday morning. Of not planning it out beforehand. Showing up to life, expectant and open to what could occur. Loyalists deserve to walk out the door in the morning and go about their day and enjoy the world around them deeply. To do that thing they've been dreaming of, without feeling guilty for being able to do it. To go after that vision, without feeling like it's not practical or productive. I'm challenging you to do this because although there is nothing wrong with wanting to live a secure and stable life, what if you risked it, responsibly, every now and again, in favor of growth? I can see you now, running and dancing in an open space—you can't believe your eyes. The grass is so bright with greens and yellows. It's almost as if you've been painted into a canvas. Even in this canvas, your figure, your dreams, who you are, is the true wonder. People flock to see it—to see your hidden essence of wildness that you're finally letting be marveled at. Don't miss out on life because of the fear. Yes, there are things in life that will be unexpected. Yes, there are things in life that will be painful. Yes, there are things in life that you will never be prepared for. But there are also things in life that you *will* be prepared for; things that are unexpectedly joyful. Surprises that aren't painful, but meaningful. Try doing something new, and out of your comfort zone, even on your own. Show yourself that you can show up, enjoy life to the fullest, and still be smart—that it's all a balance. That you know how to fend for yourself and protect yourself. But you also know how to let down your hair and dance like no one is watching. This can be as simple as starting at home. Try something new, in the comfort of your own space. Take baby steps. Fight for your right to enjoy life.

Be Proud of Being Cautious

Imagine all of the major decisions you have seen made, whether on a global, national, or personal scale, where disaster, hurt, and pain could have been avoided. Get a little annoyed. Get a little mad. It's valid. There are so many situations that would have unfolded differently if someone had listened to a Loyalist. I'm being serious. Loyalists are incredibly aware of their surroundings, the potential outcomes, the systems needed; they're inherently cautious and doubtful. And so often they are made fun of for this trait, which, honestly, the world would fall apart without if it didn't exist. Do I desire for every Loyalist to move past fear, to pursue peace, and to awaken parts of their soul that they felt like you couldn't? YES! Do I want you to change who you are, or trade it for something different? NO! The desire for growth comes from a place of knowing just how much we need healthy, flourishing Loyalists in the world. We need you to keep poking holes in plans we think will work. We need you to keep challenging us to think a little harder before taking a step. We need your input on who our decisions might affect. We need you to speak the truth when we don't want to hear it. We need to hear the reality of the situation, even the worst-case scenario sometimes. We need your unique wiring in this world, because we need fewer accidents, less heartbreak, and less carelessness. It's okay that you're wired to be affected by change, to be affected by decisions you don't agree with. Keep asking the whys. Keep seeking answers to your doubts. Keep helping us think through the choices we make. And be proud of who you are. Be proud of the impact you make by being your authentic self. We need the cautious ones. Now more than ever.

Follow Your Dreams— Whether They're Big or Small

Loyalists often desire to be noticed and seen, but this can also make them extremely uncomfortable. And with this book, my hope is that you realize you're allowed to want to be seen, and you're allowed to not want to be seen. I feel like Loyalists secretly experience shame. That if you want to be at the top, or the leader, or noticed by others, you're selfish, attention-seeking, or clueless. That if you'd prefer to stay second in command or help someone else achieve their vision with a cause you're passionate about, you're unmotivated, a sell-out, and boring. All of these characteristics can apply to either desire, and at the end of the day, they're just assumptions. I have even made these assumptions before about others! All throughout my life, I had a desire for more. I had these big dreams to become an author, to see the world, or to become a singer, or a TED Talk speaker, who made waves across the nation, helping others in their struggles, or reaching people on a large scale. The few times I spoke up about these dreams, I was shamed for them—because others thought I just wanted the attention, or that I had an inflated ego thinking I could make such a difference in the world. So I went silent about my real desires in life, and began to submit to what I thought would make me liked by others. I began to pursue what was small and practical in my life, secretly scheming on my laptop or in my journal before going to sleep. On the flip side, one of my best friends in high school had the dream of becoming a fireman. He worked nonstop to achieve this goal—he started out as a volunteer, and he began to see a lot of hard and terrible things as early as his freshman year in high school. But he was determined to keep going so that he could secure a place in the exact department and role he desired. I remember after he had graduated, and I was a senior, we spent one night at a Denny's a few towns over talking about our dreams. He went on to surprise me with the news that he did in fact get the job he had been working toward all through high school, and that he was "set." I questioned him: "Set for what? Like your whole life?" I asked. He nodded proudly. The county he was in, the way he could move up in this specific role, was exactly where he wanted to be until retirement. He was set. I attempted to celebrate with him, but I couldn't understand his desire. To want to stay in one place, one county, one department, one firehouse, for the rest of your life. He was only nineteen! How could he be satisfied with that? Looking back, I see that we had much more in common than we had in difference. We both wanted something. We both knew exactly what we wanted at a young age, and we both experienced shame for the path we were choosing to take, even by close friends and loved ones. I want to encourage you with this story, because if you know what you want in life, whether that's keeping things simple and building roots as soon as you can, or if it's to uproot everything and try to do things people told you that you couldn't, here's your permission slip to pursue whatever it is *you* desire. Although people may attempt to make you feel ashamed of what you want, or question your motives and character, know who you are and your desires well enough to let unnecessary feedback roll off your back. You're allowed to think big or think small. That's the beautiful thing about life. It unfolds in different ways for each of us. We need the big and the small.

HOW TO TAKE CARE OF
THE TYPE 6 IN YOUR LIFE

Actually Take Their Concerns
into Consideration

If you have a Type 6 in your life, know that they have a vivid internal world. They easily can imagine scenarios that tend to be the worst outcome. It may be easy for other types to unknowingly invalidate their concerns, because it either stresses them out or slows them down in some way. But one of the greatest ways you can love a Type 6 is to listen to their thoughts, ideas, and concerns, and take them seriously. Put yourself in their shoes, and seek to understand their perspective. By doing this, you can help them work out these worries hands on, and most of the time, you will actually see that they make valid points. Don't brush them off or try to hurry them up. Let Loyalists slow you down every once in a while with their questions and concerns—you'll not only make more well-rounded decisions because of it but also show them a respect that will be deeply appreciated.

Remind Them of Their
Talent and Capability

Loyalists are team players. They're usually fighting for the good of the group and filling whatever needs are necessary to help everyone else succeed. When it comes to pursuing their own voice, their own dreams, their own ideas, they have a tendency to believe that they're not actually talented, or that they're not capable of accomplishing what they desire without the help and guidance of someone else. While it is important to seek ways to become better at your passions, and to receive mentorship from someone more well-versed than you, Loyalists usually are selling themselves short. They can become blinded by what they're not, rather than become empowered for what they are. As a spouse, family member, or friend, actively take the time to encourage and empower them toward their goals. Remind them of their natural, raw talent. Believe in them fiercely, and show that belief through your actions.

Show Up for Them

I can almost guarantee that you have a Loyalist in your life who always shows up in the front row for any of your games, performances, or achievements. Type 6s are huge cheerleaders and they naturally take the position of being your biggest fan. They check in on you, they go out of their way to encourage you—behind every successful human lies a Loyalist who is doing everything they can to support you. My challenge, then, to you is to show up for them in the way they always show up for you. Check in on them. Text them first. Seek to know their goals and dreams. Get front-row seats to whatever they're involved in. Cheer for them as hard as they will cheer for you. Sacrifice for and support them the way that they always have for you. Stick by them, stay true to them. Show a reciprocated loyalty. You have no idea how loved this will make them feel.

TYPE 7

THE ENTHUSIAST

HIGH-SPIRITED, PLAYFUL, OPTIMISTIC,
FACTUAL, EAGER

CORE DESIRES:
To be free, fulfilled, unlimited, and happy

CORE FEARS:
Being without opportunity and adventure,
being trapped or stuck in pain

ULTIMATE MOTIVATIONS:
To experience life to its fullest, to avoid
things that interfere with their freedom and
happiness, to take care of themselves

AFFIRMATION:
"I will be taken care of."

Enneagram Type 7s are often thought of as the "adventurers" and "jokesters" of our world. Also known as "Enthusiasts," they are the friends who are always up for anything, and they often struggle with the fear of missing out on potential opportunities, experiences, friendships, and relationships. They are naturally inclined to live life with wander-lust, or a strong desire to travel and explore, and they not only long to live their lives to the fullest but also won't let anything stand in the way of making that happen. Enthusiasts are always evaluating and maintaining their personal freedom, and if a job, relationship, or opportunity hinders what they want to accomplish in life, they will move on to something else. Charismatic and eager, having an Enthusiast in your life guarantees that you will be pushed out of your comfort zone in the most fun and lovely way possible.

You Might Be an Enthusiast If . . .

- You hate looking at your calendar and seeing nothing fun or exciting to do.
- You always talk yourself into trying something new even if it might not be the most beneficial or realistic thing to do at the time.
- You struggle with committing to people and events, and you tend to cancel plans you had with someone if a more exciting or "worthwhile" opportunity presents itself.
- Your friends view you as the "happy" one—to the point where you feel like you can't show any other emotion around them or you'll be a disappointment.

- Although you have a hard time finishing projects, you love to brainstorm, come up with innovative ideas, and jump into things headfirst. It's not that you don't want to see something through; your mind moves so fast that moving on to something more fresh and stimulating is what keeps you sane and creative.

- You believe that taking risks, going on adventures, and experiencing the world to its fullest is what life is all about!

- You probably have played the role of the class clown at some point in your life. If a room feels too tense or uncomfortable, you feel the urge to say something lighthearted to relieve the mood.

- You tend to make decisions to maintain your freedom and happiness, even if it's not what is best for you or the people you love.

7W6 Leaning into their 6 wing, these 7s pursue adventure, but in a very grounded way. They push you to go beyond your comfort zone, but they can also be very parental. Constantly battling with their hidden need for stability and security, they tend to ignore their impulses a little bit more than 7W8s. Although they find wonder in all of the beautiful possibilities in life, they also worry about the potential outcomes of those possibilities. 7W6s are focused and concerned about their personal relationships, worrying about everyone's well-being. Since 7W6s can be prone to suppressing their well-being for the safety and comfort of others, give them a chance to let all of their built-up emotions out. Be spontaneous. Take some of their responsibilities off their plate, and help keep their wonder for life alive.

7W8

7W8s are friendly and present. They are enthusiastic and have an infectious air about them. You immediately notice when they walk into a room. Authentically bubbly and genuinely excited about life and the impact they can make in this world, life has no limits for 7W8s. Where a 7W6 may be more hesitant about change, 7W8s find a thrill in taking uncertainty and adventure head on. These 7s can sometimes be a little commanding, solely because they want the absolute most out of life and no one or nothing is going to get in their way. That being said, while staying still and putting down roots is a challenge for them, they crave the depth and community that comes from doing so more than anything. If you have a 7W8 in your life, take the pressure off them. Create a safe place for their vulnerabilities, and don't try to change them!

WHY ENTHUSIASTS NEED SELF-CARE

Enneagram Type 7s seek and run toward new horizons, even if it's at the cost of relational and experiential steadiness. Although they ultimately desire the richness that comes from a life rooted in deep relationships and passions, if the process of achieving this involves having to sit still in emotion or pain, Enthusiasts will keep on running until they tend to eventually abandon it. Because of this, they can end up living oddly rigid, scattered, and empty lives. Type 7s, you need self-care so that you can actually pursue everything your heart desires with groundedness and endurance. Through the practice of self-care and reflection, Enthusiasts will discover that they will not live trapped in pain if they stay for the heaviness. In fact, they will become stronger and more emotionally well-rounded.

SELF-CARE PRACTICES FOR TYPE 7S

Pursue a Hobby as Just a Hobby

Enthusiasts are not necessarily known for their curiosity, but they are probably the most eager and inquisitive of all the Enneagram types. Similar to our Observers, Enthusiasts want to learn all there is to know about everything, but they also want to experience what it's like to try it all out. If only they could try on every career path, every skill, etc., perhaps they would finally feel satisfied! Once Type 7s becomes intrigued by a particular topic or skill, they go all in. They do everything they can to master what has caught their attention, to the point where they can begin to think that their new hobby is now their new calling. The downfall for Enthusiasts in this situation is that a new skill or activity does eventually get old. In fact, 7s won't just grow tired of it, but when it doesn't provide the adrenaline and joy that it once did, they will find a new skill or passion almost instantaneously. This means that Type 7s have a hard time developing just one area of expertise because they have a tendency to get bored so quickly. Enthusiasts like to live life off a constant high, but when this high for a particular hobby begins to fade, what was once their "new calling" can also become a major turnoff to them. I want to mention that there is nothing wrong with becoming intrigued and excited by new activities or developing new skills. I think stimulation is something very healthy for Enthusiasts to have in their life. Where I'm challenging them is to not throw all of who they are into this new hobby, essentially, and instead let this hobby remain just that: a hobby. Don't change career paths, don't look for a new job, don't abandon everything you've done or known for a new thing you've become quickly passionate about. Slow your roll a little bit, and take the time to actually enjoy the new discovery and consider both its positives and negatives. Give this new hobby time to become a part of your life before deciding if it's really what you are now meant to do.

Face Unpleasantness Head-On

Contrary to popular belief, I've heard from a lot of Enthusiasts that some of the most sacred times in their life have been the periods when they went through a breakup or a difficult season, because these times forced them to slow down and confront their emotions head-on. Most Type 7s, I believe, feel a pressure to be continually joyful and an inspiring presence during unpleasant circumstances, instead of allowing themselves to just feel the pain they are experiencing. Allowing yourself to face hard things, not avoiding or finding a way around them, refines an Enthusiast in a unique way. As people who seek positivity and lightness in everything, feeling something unfavorable or unpleasant, and showing yourself that you can feel deeply without getting stuck in it, can change the Enthusiast's perspective entirely. It is important for them to learn that negative emotions are not necessarily negative to experience, because most of the time, they allow us to grow and even heal from current or past trauma or pain. Allowing yourself to give in to the entire spectrum of emotions also helps you develop deeper empathy for others, and can help you love and care for the people in your life in a more meaningful way.

Practice Active Listening

While Enthusiasts may not seem like "sensitive" types, they are very sensitive to anything that could potentially be negative in a conversation. While "good vibes" are very important to both Type 7s and Type 9s, Type 7s have an especially difficult time remaining present with people who might interrupt their positive mojo. Enthusiasts are usually also thinking about what they can bring to a conversation—an adventurous story, a surprising question, a hilarious joke. But entertaining and engaging others in a conversation can sometimes take the place of actually listening to what the other party has to say. While an Enthusiast may perceive a person as negative or depressing, it's important for them to remember that sometimes people simply want to connect with them by sharing their own personal experiences, whether they're positive or negative. I want Enthusiasts to realize that they can create a safe space for others to share funny and memorable stories because of the way they share their own, and giving people the same attention you expect from others will help grow your patience as well as create deeper connections with the people around you. Lean into the fact that you're incredibly quick-thinking and can come up with intentional and thought-provoking questions faster than the rest of us. Use this not just to your advantage but to better understand the people you're around.

Allow People to Slow You Down

Some consider Enthusiasts to be noncommittal and flaky, and while this can be true, I think it's important to get to the reason behind why that is. Although many believe that when Enthusiasts choose to dip out of things they had previously committed to they're doing so out of insensitivity and a lack of care, I think it goes deeper than that! Few things can drive an Enthusiast crazy, but someone coming in and slowing down their pace, or holding them back in some way, might be at the top of the list. Type 7s are constantly on the go—learning something new, going somewhere exciting, booking flights, buying a new device, trying on new clothes, taking on more hours. Freedom to be spontaneous and experimental is a means to an end for a Type 7, and the second they begin to feel overwhelmed or trapped by a particular person or obligation, it can be very hard for them to follow through with what they've committed to, especially when something that appears to be more fun hangs in the balance. Type 7s in fact do care very deeply about people and causes, but they care about their freedom more. This is because out of everything in life, they fear missing out on something the most. They fear getting stuck in conflict, stuck in negative emotions, stuck in things that they don't want to do. As much as Enthusiasts pursue risk and discomfort in terms of adventure, they avoid risk and discomfort emotionally and relationally at all costs. I believe that all the Enneagram types can meet Enthusiasts in the middle, but I believe Enthusiasts can meet us in the middle as well. There is a huge chance for growth on the edge of seemingly negative experiences or emotions—and though even reading this is probably physically painful for you as a Type 7, it is *through* the realness of your emotional experience that you will reach the satisfaction you are searching for everywhere else. So allow that person who genuinely wants to voice their feelings to you to do so, or go to that event you committed to that now seems anything but enjoyable, because there are often other people involved in your decisions, whether you actively include them or not. Choosing to deepen your relationships and connection to causes, even if it appears to be painful, may actually lead to a sense of fulfillment that lasts.

Try Planning Things Out

Continuing the theme of Enthusiasts fearing being limited or confined, most Type 7s actively decide against planning anything in their life. They are incredibly aware of the endless possibilities of the present and the future, and they would rather go about each day with the flexibility to pursue one of those possibilities at the drop of the hat. This can sometimes lead to Enthusiasts leaving their friends, or those counting on them, hanging in the balance of their spontaneity. The decisions or plans that need to be made or set in stone can lead to extreme mental stress for our Type 7s. They either make decisions flippantly or they become paralyzed by the thought of making the wrong decision. Enthusiasts just want to be happy and to make sure that others are happy, too, and so choosing an outcome that might negatively affect either party is, for them, the most frightening position to be in. I hate to break it to you, Enthusiasts, but no matter which option is chosen, a negative conversation, emotion, or experience might occur. Where there are humans involved, there will always be someone you might disappoint, something you have to do that isn't fun, a serious conversation that needs to be had—but that's part of what makes life beautiful. The balance of light and heavy is what makes the light so memorable and amazing. So I want to encourage you to buy a planner. That's right, I said it. I want you to buy a planner. Or download a planner app on your phone. I want you to schedule those meetings. RSVP to that event. Text or call that person to have that conversation you've been putting off. Add the things on your calendar that are indeed unavoidable at the moment. Schedule a period of time to get done what you need to get done. Then block out an hour or two each day to do something fun. You don't have to plan out what it is you're going to do, but treat yourself every day to being spontaneous. Life is all about finding a balance!

Let Your Smile Have a Day Off

Many Enthusiasts we know are the life of the party. They walk into a room, and things are just better. They make things fun and pleasant. Their energy and charisma is contagious, and you can't help but feel happy and entertained when you're around them. Because Enthusiasts are optimistic by nature, they've kind of stepped into this role unintentionally. But with this pressure comes a responsibility that we don't often realize weighs heavily on them. Type 7s can become the thermostat of our groups, organizations, and relationships—we rely on them to turn up the laugher and light, to bring the positive, upbeat outlook to every situation, every single time, even if they may not feel like it. We rely on them to be charming in the face of negativity or tension, when they're being just as affected by whatever is going on as we are. I've titled this self-care tip "Let Your Smile Have a Day Off" because, Enthusiasts, you deserve to take time away from this pressure. You are not loved solely because you're positive, you are not loved solely because you're the life of the party, you are loved because of who you are—your voice, your quirks, your heart, your passion, your flaws. You are loved for all of you.

Say "No" to Really Say "Yes"

While Enthusiasts fight the same battle as other Enneagram types who struggle with saying no to the demands and desires of others, they also have a deeper tension within them that affects their ability to even say no to themselves. Enthusiasts not only fear being trapped or limited by others but they're also afraid of limiting themselves or slowing down. When a Type 7 has an impulse to buy something, go somewhere, or try out something new, for example, they usually don't want to tell themselves "no." They have a fear of missing out on the full wonder of a moment, and Enthusiasts want the complete experience. To avoid the feeling of deprivation, they can sometimes resort to indulging in things—food, travel, whatever they love—in excess. One of the most challenging, but vital, self-care exercises a Type 7 can do is to sometimes just say no to their whims and impulses. To not get the coffee at the coffee shop while they're studying. To not say yes to another night out or to another weekend getaway. The hard part here is Enthusiasts have to realize that although they are saying no to something, they are actually saying yes to other things. They're saying yes to rest. Saying yes to understanding themselves better. Saying yes to being more present in a relationship. Saying yes to the inner needs they have that often go unfulfilled. Enthusiasts need to know that it's okay to not be invited and it's okay to say no. It's okay that things are happening without you, and it's a freeing thing to be released from the grip of chasing everything and everyone that's exciting. It's okay to take care of yourself. It's okay to say no. Because you're actually saying yes!

Get Quiet Every Day

Enthusiasts crave stimulation, whether that's through music, books, TV, movies, YouTube, TikTok, video games, podcasts, you name it. Even during their moments of rest, there is usually some kind of noise going on in their mind or in the background. Type 7s, as scary as it may be for you, one of the best self-care practices you can develop is the art of getting quiet. Every night or morning, I encourage you to dedicate a chunk of time to being completely still and silent with your thoughts. I know that may sound terrifying, and to be honest, it might be the first time you've ever truly done it, but don't put too much pressure on yourself before you try it. You only need to sit still and close your eyes for a few minutes. Then try turning it into something you do every day, and slowly build up the time as you become more comfortable. This meditation-type practice will better connect you to your current emotions and surroundings—which 7s often neglect to do.

Allow Those Who Love You to Know You

I have a little group chat that I created on Instagram a few months ago specifically for Type 7s. The members of the group chat are essentially all strangers, but I will occasionally pop in and ask questions that are specific to their type so I can better understand them while also making my content more accurate. One day, we began discussing Enthusiasts within friendships, and I asked them, "What does it take for a 7 to open up to others?" In my personal experience, I had always felt like I didn't know my Type 7 friends that well—or at least felt that it was difficult to connect with them on an emotional level. The answers I received were incredibly interesting. Most of the Enthusiasts in the chat said that a lot of people assume they are close with them because of how naturally outgoing they are. They tend to collect a lot of friendships, when they usually have only one or two people they would consider their close friends. It is difficult for them to let others truly know them because they fear any potential commitment or negativity that could come from the interaction. And even within those one or two close friendships, showing up with their emotions can be difficult because they don't ever want to come across as negative. An Enthusiast needs to realize that there are people in their life that genuinely want to know them, and that their pain is not negative or a burden to others; rather, it's an important part of connecting with them. I challenge Enthusiasts to let those that love you know you. Like, really know you. All of the tears, complaints, frustrations, and more. This will not pollute your relationships, it will strengthen them.

Be Okay with Needing Help

Enthusiasts at their core long to be taken care of above all else, though they would never let you know this. Type 7s are naturally self-sufficient and would prefer to not bother others with their needs. Growing up, many Enthusiasts most likely felt a level of responsibility to keep everyone and themselves happy. They may have even felt pressure to amuse and entertain themselves to stave off any potential conflict. Because even though Enthusiasts come across as fearless, they're actually motivated by fear. That being said, what I want Enthusiasts to know is that it's okay to need help. And it's okay to break down. It's okay to feel sadness. It's okay to be affected by something that hurts you. It's okay to need assistance in the face of something or someone that challenges you. A huge part of saying no to your impulses is saying yes to the community. Saying yes to letting others in. Yes, people love you because you are positive, but you are worth more than your happiness. You are worth more than what you can offer to others. You are a full, whole human being, with a spectrum of feelings and preferences. And it's okay to dig deep, to get in touch with those desires, and even to express them toward others. You don't have to go this alone. You are not letting anyone down by asking for help. You are not weaker for it, and it doesn't make you "soft."

Listen to Those Who Love You

I can't imagine the amount of times people have told you to "chill" or "slow down." And it likely annoys you, too, because constantly hearing "do nothing" or that "you should really slow down more" makes you feel misunderstood, and it makes you want to slow down even less. While I do think some people can say those things out of jealousy or with ill-intent, it's important to take stock of the people who are earnestly telling you that it's time to relax. If the people who are saying these things to you are the people you consider yourself to be closest with, individuals who have proved to be on your team no matter what, as annoying as it may be, it might be time to take their suggestions to heart. No matter what your Enneagram type is, we all have trouble objectively assessing our actions. That's the whole beauty of finding a community of people you love and trust. I've learned throughout the years that the people who love you the most ultimately want what's best for you—even if it means they risk saying something that you don't want to hear. Risking the relationship because they want to see you thrive . . . hold those people tightly! Because they see beyond your bubbly, positive exterior to a whole, healing person. All of this being said, Enthusiasts are often doing so many things at once that they sometimes don't even realize *why* they are doing those things. They can lose sight of their inner motivations. They can lose sight of what actually matters. But giving yourself the space to do nothing, and working through the guilt or fear you experience by sitting still, will only aid your growth as a human. There's no one way to effectively do this, either. Find a way to slow down and be still that simply works best for you.

Feel So You Can Process

The Enthusiast is perhaps the Enneagram type that dislikes feeling sadness, hurt, anger, frustration, and laziness the most. While the other types don't particularly enjoy those emotions either, Type 7s feel ashamed to be experiencing such negative emotions when they could just choose to be happy. There is a sense of guilt they feel when they are affected by the harsh and hurtful things in this world. And there is also a sense of fear they feel—such as by thinking, *What if I will never be able to escape this feeling?* The truth is, trying to outrun your feelings only brings you closer to becoming imprisoned by them. Although on the outside you may look free, you probably don't feel free, which is why it's important for Enthusiasts to understand that we don't just feel emotions for the sake of it. If you've ever been to therapy or have known someone who has gone, you may know that therapists often encourage you to allow yourself to feel things deeply so that you can ultimately get to the other side of them. My therapist throughout our time together has always reminded me that "the only way out is through." The only way out of feeling trapped or stuck by emotions that scare you is to feel them. We feel so we can process. We process so we can move on. So rather than viewing sadness or apathy as a force that will overtake you, look at it as a missing puzzle piece from the full picture. You will be sobered by the pain, but this will allow you to live in the fully awake and alive way you're always seeking. True joy and satisfaction will only come out of the process. There's no rushing through it, avoiding it, or short-changing it.

Include Someone in Your Adventures

While I think that most Enthusiasts often want to include others in their impulsive plans, I do think that sometimes a spontaneous adventure is actually an act of self-defense and self-preservation for a Type 7. It's a way to let go of the chance of someone staining the magical expectations they are trying to meet in their experiences. In other words, not going on adventures with others is less of a hassle in a Type 7's eyes. You don't have to worry about someone else's opinions or preferences or expectations . . . not just of the adventure you're going on but also of you! However, life is all about finding balance, right? It's important to hike alone, but it's also important to invite others into your spontaneity. It's important to be free from the expectations of others, but it's also important to feel that you matter to someone, and that you can affect them as much as they affect you. Your fear of the experience not being all you had hoped it to be because someone else is there with you may exist, but, most likely, the experience will exceed your expectations when someone you love is there to enhance it. Their suggestion, their preference, their expectation might actually be the stimulation and excitement that makes everything better. Not only that, but a conversation, light or heavy, may make the experience not only thrilling but also richer.

Don't Be Afraid of Putting Down Roots

While the idea of having roots is comforting to some, it can be a terrifying thought to an Enthusiast. Staying in the same place, with the same people, eating the same food, seeing the same things over and over and over again could even be considered equivalent to living in a circle of hell. Security for Type 7s can often sound like restriction and limitation, which they spend most of their life trying to avoid. If there is anything you've learned about Enthusiasts in this book, it's probably that their thirst for new experiences can seemingly never be quenched. But one of the greatest forms of self-care for someone who believes everything exciting is always happening somewhere else is intentionally taking the time to stay in one place. Take on your fear of stagnancy by being stagnant for a change. I believe that when Enthusiasts take the time to put down roots wherever they have been placed at this moment in time, they will begin to see they have been missing out on an unexplained richness that can only occur when they are still. They will find that true contentment with their people, their season, their current residence, and other things in their life comes from within themselves—and that contentment is not only a choice but a practice. A practice of waking up and going against what comes naturally. Going against the running. Going against the escaping. Deciding to stay in one place for a full year, or two years. At the same job. In the same friend group. Showing yourself that you can find contentment with whatever is in front of you will help you thirst for life in a healthy way. As an Enthusiast, take some time to let your roots grow deep for a little bit. You will be pleasantly surprised.

Less Is More

Both Type 4s and Type 7s live their lives with a constant sense of longing. In fact, many Type 7s can misidentify their Enneagram number because of the Enthusiast's and Individualist's shared desire for the finer things in life, as well as their ability to dream big and explore all possibilities. What distinguishes the two types from one another, however, is what each one is longing for. Individualists tend to long for something different—something that they used to have, something they don't have, something they wish to have. This sense of longing usually comes from a place of feeling as though they are lacking something essential, and without this one thing, they will never be complete or "normal." For Enthusiasts, however, this sense of longing is focused on a desire for *more*. Whatever it is, Enthusiasts want the most of it—not to be the best, but because they desire to feel fulfilled. This becomes an endless pursuit for them, because everything they chase provides only a temporary high or satisfaction, which is how this continuous desire to do or have more is fueled. Enthusiasts were born with or nurtured to believe that more is always better. And when things begin to feel unsafe, out of control, or overwhelming, this impulse to buy more, eat more, shop more, exercise more, work more, travel more, whatever it may be, arises in them and it arises powerfully. A self-care challenge I have for Enthusiasts involves the concept of minimalism—being less of a consumer, purchasing and seeking long-term, sustainable things, and developing a minimalistic state of heart. This means believing that everything you have and everyone you love is enough for you to be satisfied right now in this moment. There is nothing you are missing to be found out there—no new friendship, relationship, view, or event will make you feel more satisfied in the long run than you do right now. It's all right to feel a little low every now and then because all highs are indeed temporary. There is nothing to fear in the lowness. You will be okay.

HOW TO TAKE CARE OF THE TYPE 7 IN YOUR LIFE

Give Them the Freedom to Dream

If you have a Type 7 in your life, you know that they are idea machines. They are constantly envisioning and dreaming up adventures, business plans, parties, and more. A lot of people find their thirst for opportunity to be exhausting, and it can often be misinterpreted as Enthusiasts making concrete plans and decisions because they are not satisfied with their current life. But although satisfaction is something they're constantly chasing and struggling to maintain, it can also be Enthusiasts' greatest strength—because Enthusiasts don't just want the most fulfilling and happy life for themselves, they want it for you as well. They want to push you and help you get to new heights—heights that you never thought you could reach. To give you a better look into the Enthusiast's mind, envision a hamster running furiously on a wheel . . . now imagine it never getting off. A Type 7's mind is never not brewing, thinking, or conjuring up something new. Type 7s literally can't help it. And one of the best things that you can do for them as their friend or loved one is to give them the space to explore these thoughts and creative ideas. They will go crazy if they can't get them out somehow. Understand that once a Type 7 starts talking about how cool it would be to live in Germany, they're most likely *just* talking about how cool it would be to live in Germany. Most of the time, Enthusiasts talk about how cool or how dreamy something could be, not because they want to do it or are unsatisfied, but simply because it's fun to imagine the possibilities. Dream with them. Imagine with them. Challenge yourself by being swept up with them every so often.

Create a Safe Space for Them

Enthusiasts are doers and dreamers . . . they're not usually the deepest of feelers. As a friend or partner of an Enthusiast, I'm sure that sometimes you feel as though you never know what they're actually feeling—that they're only showing you half of what is going on inside their mind—which, in a sense, is true. I think it's important for others to understand that Enthusiasts who are not on a path to self-awareness are just as clueless about their emotions as you are. There is no magic formula or recipe to get an Enthusiast to describe the depths of what they feel, because they have been moving too fast to even be aware of how they feel. The more you try to change this about them, the more distance they will create between you. My advice would be to approach them with positivity and empathy. Create a safe space for them to open up. Plan a surprise experience with them. Do something spontaneous for them. Match their pace. Show them that you're there. And give them time. Give them the

time to trust you. They will notice and appreciate the effort you are making to understand them. And once they see that you want what's best for
them, they'll feel better about opening up.

Take Them Seriously

Are Enthusiasts goofballs? Yes. Are they constantly spitting out ideas,
jokes, or dreams? Yes. Are they easily excited about beautiful and fun
things? Yes. Does this mean they aren't serious about their goals and
passions? Heck no. Enthusiasts are just as much intellectuals as they are
entertainers, and their ability to retain and process information is unparalleled. I once read an article about how Type 7s have the most potential
to be creative geniuses, and I couldn't agree more. If you have an Enthusiast on your team or in your life, learn about their passions. Take their
suggestions and ideas seriously. Because out of the thousands they're
dreaming up every day, there are probably more than one hundred that
are game-changers for your business, your friendship, or your life. Every
Type 7 I have met has been both incredibly book and street smart. They
know how to work hard, and they know how to play hard. Rather than
making them feel guilty for being good at both, take the time to learn
from them once in a while. Take their way of life and their ideas seriously,
because it matters to them, and it may enliven your life, too!

TYPE 8

THE CHALLENGER

STRONG-WILLED, RESOURCEFUL,
CONFIDENT, PROTECTIVE, ASSERTIVE

CORE DESIRES:

To take charge of their life, to be strong,
to defend themselves and others

CORE FEARS:

Being at the mercy of someone else,
being hurt or taken advantage of

ULTIMATE MOTIVATIONS:

To demonstrate their strength,
to maintain self-reliance and composure,
to overcome weakness

AFFIRMATION:

"I will not be betrayed."

Enneagram Type 8s are our warrior-like friends, family members, and coworkers. When they walk into a room, they have an authoritative air about them that cannot be ignored. These folks love others in big ways, and they also do big things. Type 8s, also known as Challengers, will usually find themselves being placed in leadership roles very quickly because of the level of dedication and assertiveness they bring to every situation. They are naturally authoritative and strongly dislike others being in control of what they do. Challengers are not afraid to rock the boat and ask hard questions. They are the ones continually fighting for the underdog, because secretly they see the underdog within themselves. Type 8s give everyone a fighting chance, and if you have one in your life, you know that they will always fight for you and protect you.

You Might Be a Challenger If . . .

- You don't mind confrontation. In fact, the occasional debate makes you come alive a little bit inside.
- You like to show others that they are more than they give themselves credit for.
- You prefer to be in charge and take the lead so things actually get done.
- You feel as though it is your duty to be a pillar of strength for others.
- You tend to push yourself beyond your physical and mental limits to see how far you can go.
- Others don't realize how soft you are inside because of your tough exterior.
- People have told you that you "come on really strong,"

and can even be "intimidating" or "too much" at times.

- You shield yourself from vulnerability through stimulating activity and responsibility.
- You have a hard time justifying rest and stillness to yourself.
- Processing emotion is very difficult for you, and it usually takes you a long time to figure things out in that way.
- Your gut reaction to upsetting situations is anger first, true emotions second.
- You cannot stand to see injustice in the world or in the lives of your loved ones.

8W7

With a wing 7, Type 8s show up in the world as outgoing go-getters who think literally *nothing* is impossible! They have many dreams, and somehow they accomplish them all. Their intensity cannot be matched, and underneath their authoritative presence they have an affectionate, tender heart. They're down for anything! 8W7s will protect and fight for you enthusiastically . . . join them in taking the world by storm!

8W9

Type 8s that lean into their 9 wing show up a little more nonchalantly in the world. They are still natural leaders but are more aware of how their intensity may affect others. Their love for confrontation is matched with a need for harmony; they will confront you, but they usually are not enjoying it. 8W9s realize more often than other 8s when they need to slow down, and they're more prone to listening intentionally. They are the gentle giants you need in your life!

WHY CHALLENGERS NEED SELF-CARE

Type 8s are prone to pushing themselves beyond their limits, even to the point of serious physical and mental exhaustion. Challengers want to believe they are superhuman, because they feel the weight of staying on top of things so intensely. But Type 8s are unfortunately subject to their own human nature and can experience a physical and/or emotional hurt to the point where they cannot ignore it anymore. Challengers need self-care so that they can learn how to continually access their tenderness in a rhythmic and consistent manner and can begin to show up for their responsibilities and loved ones with presence and intentionality. Learning to understand and sit in these difficult emotions by practicing self-care also helps Type 8s develop a healthier relationship with change. Self-care allows the Challenger to let go of always being in charge, and instead let others in. When they are self-aware, Challengers become incredibly poised and helpful leaders who deeply believe in candor and generosity.

SELF-CARE PRACTICES FOR TYPE 8S

Don't Be Afraid of Counseling

As I was writing this little book, I was able to talk to and engage with a lot of different Challengers about habits or patterns they have that ended up changing their lives for the better. When I saw that every single Type 8 I talked to mentioned counseling, I knew I had to include it. Don't be afraid of counseling. Most Challengers that I've had the pleasure of knowing have lived a hard life in some way. Challengers may have been told to toughen up, to be strong . . . or someone betrayed their trust, exploited their weakness, which led them to develop their core fear: being harmed or taken advantage of. Going to a trusted professional to help validate and process any sort of trauma that you went through, big or small, regardless of your Enneagram type, is one of the best investments you can make with regard to self-care. Even if you think you have never experienced something incredibly "hard," it's okay to not be okay. It's okay to admit that you need to heal or recover or process anything. Know that you can do so with a trained professional, someone who won't mind your questions and concerns.

Know You Are More Than Your Passion

Challengers are known for their feistiness. They have strong opinions and they are not afraid to share them with others. Their fierceness goes unmatched, and often Challengers develop an identity around their ability to be tough and courageous. But sometimes it can seem like Challengers have only one state of being: intensity. The reality is, underneath all of their passion and ferocity is a tender, thoughtful heart that often gets buried by the pressure to be strong. I believe that all the Challengers of this world need to know they are more than just their passion. So, Challengers, if no one has ever told you this before, I want you to know that, yes, we love your strength, but you are not loved solely for it. We love your tenacity, but your value is not dependent on that. You are free to be yourself. You are free to be passionate. You are free to explore your entire emotional being without shame or fear. What you offer the world goes beyond your strength and passion; it goes deep within who you are. Learn to embrace every weakness and feeling you have; you are beautiful!

Continue to Pursue Knowledge

Challengers like to be on top of things. They like to feel as if they're moving forward in their life, and they will do whatever is necessary to achieve their goals. Challengers will learn and push until they feel as though they are on top. They have no problem believing they're experts on what they're passionate about, or that they have the most to offer others as opposed to the other way around. They gravitate toward adding more obstacles and challenges to their life to add more stimulation. But because of this inner drive, they can prevent themselves from learning even more about what they're keenly interested in. While they crave this constant conquering, they tend to choose the paths of things that they know they can conquer. They live in a circle of what makes them feel strong. Challengers' fear of being seen as weak—and, frankly, their pride—can keep them from seeing the value in being a continual student. My encouragement for Challengers is to take time to not just challenge those who know more than you or who disagree with you but to listen to them. And even if out of the ten things they talk about, you learn only one thing, it's worth it! Find excitement in the fact that reaching the top never actually happens; we just choose when we've reached the top. Find thrill in the pursuit of knowledge—not to challenge others with it, but to simply have it.

Start Setting Boundaries

Challengers can struggle with becoming overwhelmed by all of their obligations and tend to complain about how they simply don't have time to take a break. They can become oblivious to the fact that when faced with the thousand opportunities they have to be leaders, they indeed have a choice in the matter. Challengers, whether or not they will admit it, despise saying no. They are not necessarily people-pleasers, but people who would rather say yes and be stressed than appear as if they are weak and can't handle the responsibility, even if taking on this responsibility is not what's best for them. Because the practice of setting boundaries does not come naturally to them, Challengers can often let things like communicating with family members, fostering friendships and relationships, and anything that does not have to do with what they're focused on juggling fall to the wayside. So for all of my overcommitted, burnt-out Challengers, know that boundaries are your friend. Saying no is not weak; in fact, it can be the strongest and healthiest thing you can do. If someone loses their respect for you because you were bold and brave enough to say no, it is not your job to prove them wrong. Take responsibility for your mental, emotional, physical, and spiritual health, because it matters. And the need to take care of your innate human nature does not make you weak; it actually demands respect from others. You'll love yourself and the people in your life much more passionately and fervently when you start setting up the boundaries that are right for you.

Take Up Space

One of the hardest personal things that Challengers have to go through is the feeling of being "too much." Many Type 8s, as you've learned, are quite intense people. They walk into a room and you know that they have entered because they are authentic, larger-than-life souls. But unfortunately, they are often shamed for being the way they are. This happens with both sexes, but especially with female Challengers. Female Challengers go after life with tenacity, unafraid and bold. This can often be extremely intimidating for males or even other females. Challengers can be stereotyped as jerks and bullies simply because they tend to live life in an honest way. It is difficult to be wired in a way that many people aren't ready for yet. And I want to take this little section of the book to say: that is not your problem. While becoming self-aware is important, and learning how our energy affects others is similarly important, that goes for every single Enneagram type, not just Challengers. I know you may not be the biggest fan of obtaining permission, but I'm giving it to you anyway: You're allowed to walk into a room and be proud of who you are. You are not "too much" for others. In fact, we need healthy Challengers to take up more space in this world. We need your intuition and justice-focused mind. In a time when the world is finally awakening to the idea that it's okay to be different and to not fit the mold of what others expect, we need healthy Challengers to be leading the movement. So walk into the room with confidence, and help us gain our confidence, too. Take up space, unashamedly.

Go on a Cry Run

My best friend from childhood is an Enneagram Type 8. I call her my fearless friend. She's the one who always reminds me of my worth and value. The one who asks the server to fix my order at a restaurant if it comes out wrong. She is the friend who has always had something going on because in any club or extracurricular activity she joined, she quickly became the one in charge, usually without even trying. She wasn't afraid to talk to boys. She was quick to point out someone taking advantage of me when I couldn't see it. She felt a duty to keep her family and friends safe, while handling an unreal amount of pressure on her shoulders with both strength and dignity. I always wondered how she did it all—because she really seemed to be able to go through life without showing any sense of weakness. One day at her house, she asked me if we could go on a run around the neighborhood. As we were running, she confided in me about this practice she does called "cry runs." In the heat of uncertainty, in the heat of the moment, in the heat of unimaginable pressure, she says she goes outside, begins running, and just sobs. The reason why I'm sharing this story is because I wanted to tell you two important things. The first is: Challengers, try going on a cry run. It will be okay. You're allowed to feel the weight or heaviness of something. You're allowed to need time and space to process. Use a cry run not just to regain control but to let yourself feel deeply. Second, find someone to cry-run with. Once I learned about Challengers' struggle with being vulnerable even around their loved ones, I felt so honored that my dear friend would choose *me* to cry-run with. I felt like she wanted me to be a part of her life in a meaningful way. I know it can be scary to let people in like that, but if they've proven to be trustworthy, you have nothing to be afraid of. So go ahead, ask them on a cry run.

Explore What's Underneath Your Anger

Challengers are reactive people, which means that the first emotion they usually feel is anger. No matter what the situation is—no matter the person, big or small—Type 8's natural and instinctive emotion is anger. This doesn't necessarily mean they are violent or aggressive, but when Challengers lack self-awareness or they are in a state of stress, they don't explore the root cause of the anger they feel. Because even though Challengers may believe that they are just angry or impassioned people, it actually goes way deeper than that. Underneath the anger lies the true emotion they are experiencing, and it takes a moment of stepping back and processing to understand there is something more beneath the surface. I feel as though many Challengers get stereotyped as angry people when in reality they're not. They're in touch with their anger, sure, but it's often masking their authentic emotions. So I encourage Challengers to ask themselves, "What is underneath this anger?" Take a step back, analyze the situation, and maybe even let someone else in to ask the question "What is underneath?" You are more than your anger, and your deep passion is there for a reason. Take some time to explore it and stay in touch with it.

Stay Within Your Limits

Type 3s, Type 7s, and Type 8s are considered to be the three most "aggressive" types within the Enneagram, because they are all predominantly motivated to take action before processing their emotions. They're shoot-and-then-aim kind of people. And Challengers are especially known for having the most energy of all the types, so slowing their pace is extremely difficult for them—not necessarily because they don't want to relax or rest, but because they don't see themselves as people who need to slow down that often. They see themselves as having an endless amount of energy, and it is hard for them to recognize when they've reached their limits. To a Challenger, there are no physical limits, just obstacles to overcome. However, Type 8s also need to learn how to become aware of their human needs. Because as much as they might ignore them, they're not going to go away. Limits do not make us weak; they make us human. And sometimes it is within limits that we discover our creativity and innovation. I think it's a beautiful thing to understand your limits, because they help you understand that you need other people, and even though that can be a difficult concept for most Challengers to grasp, staying within your limits allows you to improve, enrich, and benefit your life.

Slow Your Mornings, Afternoons, and Evenings

As a breather from all of this heavy information, I want to discuss the beauty of slow mornings for a Type 8. Here are your instructions: Wake up an hour before you usually do, or set aside your responsibilities an hour before you normally would. Do a skin care routine if you have one and take five minutes to breathe. Grab your favorite cup of coffee or tea—although I would recommend decaf if you're choosing to do this in the evening—and light a few candles. Put on your favorite playlist or sit in silence. Find a cozy corner in your house, perhaps near a window, or on your porch or in your backyard. Make the next twenty to thirty minutes whatever you want them to be, but preferably, allow yourself to not be stimulated by anything except your own thoughts and surroundings. Bring a journal if you're comfortable with that, or use a camera to take photos of things that are inspiring to you in that moment. Grow into your wild and restful self through experiencing the ambiance. Challengers aren't completely concerned with aesthetics, so giving yourself the space to try out different styles and rhythms to help you find a slow routine that's cozy for you is key.

Choose Empathy

Challengers are justice-oriented. They are always fighting for the underdog, and they strongly believe in fairness. With this, though, comes a tendency to believe that "it's my way or the highway!" Meaning, Challengers believe that their way of living and seeing the world is not only the correct way but the just way. When they come across people who disagree with them, they have no problem standing up for what they believe in, which is extremely admirable. However, when their desire to be right takes over their ability to empathize, self-growth is inhibited. As I previously mentioned, Challengers are always cheering for the underdog. Sometimes it's to offer playful encouragement, but most of the time it's because they genuinely want to see those who are struggling the most finally succeed—they feel as though this is their own inner narrative as well. So Challengers have enormous space for empathy in their hearts; they just carefully choose whom to give it to. That being said, a great way for Challengers to nurture their personal growth would be to extend empathy to those they feel are in opposition to them, to those they perceive as antagonists. Once Challengers begin to do this, they will realize that, despite their differences with others, everyone is worth giving a fair chance. So, Challengers, I encourage you to allow different perspectives—even if you disagree with them—to impact you and to expand your view of the world.

Get Flexible

All right, Challengers, you always tell everyone else like it is, and I would say you expect that in return. So I am here to be unapologetically honest with you . . . you can be kind of inflexible sometimes! When you have a plan, goal, or expectation in your mind, you will not let anyone or anything get in your way. Challengers sometimes tend to bulldoze others, or to flat-out ignore what they want, to maintain control of their plan and destiny. While their resoluteness can be an admirable trait, it can also become unhealthy when a Challenger begins to fight against anything in their life that may jeopardize their plans. Dealing with change is extremely difficult for Type 8s, perhaps more than for any other type— because once they settle into a pattern or routine, or they've learned to trust certain friends or coworkers, and then everything gets flipped upside down, it can be quite a disorienting experience for a Challenger. This is why it's important for a Challenger's mental health to accept that change is inevitable—and that it's not always going to hurt you. Sometimes change is the best and healthiest thing you can experience in your situation. Just as you would become more physically flexible over time by doing stretching exercises, learning to spiritually go with the flow takes time as well. I want to make it clear that these words are not in an effort to change who you are; your questions and concerns are valid in light of change. I am encouraging you to try out flexibility within your plans and opinions solely to foster more inner growth, because you can be alarmed by change and still be able to adapt to it. So the next time you're upset about something that is going against your will, try testing your flexibility.

Be Intentionally Unproductive

Yikes! I probably just terrified all of the Challengers with that statement. Every Type 8 I've met in my life has unparalleled charisma and the drive to get everything they want out of life. They are constantly working, moving on to the next thing, busying themselves with a new hobby, or overcoming a new obstacle. In a way, I think doing these things brings many Challengers joy. They are very physical people, and having external stimulation is important for their sanity. However, this can get out of hand if it's not managed, so Challengers, I want you to think of the last time you truly did nothing—not just *did* nothing but *chose* to do nothing intentionally. For many of you, I imagine this was a very difficult thing to recall. But I want you to entertain this thought for a bit longer, because I want to give you an assignment. Choose an upcoming weekend or weekday, whatever works best for you, and dedicate this day to just being—not tackling a new project or scheduling every hour with a new activity. Call this day whatever you want—maybe it can be your own version of "Self-Care Sunday"—but consider it sacred. Nothing and no one can get in the way of this self-care day; it is your much-needed time to be intentionally unproductive.

Practice Prayer or Meditation

Whatever their religious or spiritual beliefs, I have witnessed the most radical self-growth happen in all of the Enneagram types, and especially Challengers, through the practice of contemplative prayer and meditation. Without sounding like a broken record, it's important to understand how much Challengers need to understand the art of slowing down. Opening themselves up to experience the surrender that comes with prayer or meditation reconciles a Challenger's fear of being at the mercy of someone else. And though this fear is valid, Challengers must remember that life cannot be perfectly controlled no matter how hard they try. Things will always happen that are not within their power. People will always be different from what they expected, in both good ways and bad. Plans may not go as they had hoped. But through realizing it's okay to be affected by the waves of change and that it brings us to a place of understanding how fragile plans, relationships, and life can be, we're able to live on the offense as opposed to on the defense. Rather than trying to protect themselves and everyone else from the inevitable, Challengers can accept it, surrender to the things they cannot control, and learn to take up daily practices of gratitude instead.

Be Mutually Open and Vulnerable

As a Challenger, you may find there are patterns in your relationships. People will seek to be vulnerable with you, but despite this a sense of disconnection can still exist between you and them. You may hear what the other person is telling you, and encourage openness in your friendship with said person, but you're likely not engaging in the openness yourself. A huge self-care tip for Challengers is to practice being mutually open and vulnerable with those you care about. Challengers have a tendency to either give too much or take too much. They want to be "all-in" in their relationships, but are also prone to leaving one foot out of them just in case they get hurt. Challengers have a hard time finding the balance and rhythm to the give-*and*-take aspect of relationships, which is why it's important for them to develop mutual vulnerability, where they can communicate when they need to take, and can show up for someone else when they are in need of help. Don't be afraid to tear down those walls within yourself. You have learned a lot about the importance of being vulnerable in this chapter, but it's because it's key for Challengers to get in touch with on their journey toward self-discovery. Challengers, I want you to know that it's okay to give, and it's okay to rely on others. It's okay to be dependent, and it's okay to encourage independence. Both of your "all-in" desires can live in harmony; it just may take some practice to balance them!

Let Others Tell You
What to Do for a Change

Allowing themselves to be told what to do is a practice that will be quite hard for most Challengers to master, because many of them have a complicated relationship with authority. They don't like to be forced to follow rules; they want to make their own rules. Even if others' rules are of the same caliber as their own, Challengers want to feel assured that the rules are of their choosing. This stems from their fear of being at the mercy of somebody else's decision-making. But, Challengers, although this is not always the case, what if sometimes someone else actually knows what is best for you? I know it's a crazy thought, but everyone, regardless of Enneagram type, struggles to see outside themselves and their tendencies every now and then, which is why we need others to occasionally push us in the direction that will lead to our healthiest and most whole self. Sometimes we get so caught up in what we *think* is best that we miss what actually *is* best. There is a lot I could unpack here, but strategic growth for a Challenger starts with learning to accept authority—accepting that sometimes other people know better than you, and sometimes they don't. Yes, there are a lot of leaders who don't know what they're doing, but there are also a lot of leaders who do, perhaps even more than you do. Take the time to learn from the leaders and mentors whom you admire. Allow them to influence your life a little bit. Challengers have an incredible intuition, and won't have a problem distinguishing between right and wrong, so trust that gut. Take a chance on the wisdom of someone else. It just might surprise you.

HOW TO TAKE CARE OF THE TYPE 8 IN YOUR LIFE

Be Kind to Them in Conflict

If you have a Type 8 in your life, you know that they are confrontational individuals. They are constantly thinking of ways they can keep testing the status quo, and they're unafraid to tell someone what they think to their face. A lot of people look at these actions and see insensitivity or cruelty, and Challengers can often be misunderstood as people who are always seeking to fight or debate others. While this is partly true, as Challengers are always prepared for a moment of conflict, that doesn't mean they always enjoy it. Challengers usually feel a sense of responsibility to be the first ones to take a stand in times of conflict because they want to be strong for themselves and for the people they care about. In fact, I believe Challengers' passion for confrontation comes from a place of despising it so much that they would rather just get it over with so everyone, including them, can move on. Challengers want to lay it all out on the table and work it out with you, and even though they may appear fearless, engaging in conflict can still be a difficult task for them. So be kind in conflict with your Challenger. You can do this by bringing the same level of honesty and authenticity to the conversation, or showing that you are committed to finding a solution. Your Challenger might not want you to think they are affected by your words or actions, but they deeply desire harmony and trust within any type of friendship or relationship they have. Remember their strong desire for conflict resolution is not really about wanting to fight but wanting everything to be okay again.

Accept Their Intensity

For any personality or Enneagram type, feeling like someone thinks you'd be better off different from the way you're wired can be the worst feeling in the world. Challengers continually feel a pressure to change who they are, because who they are takes over a room pretty quickly. People either like it or they don't, and Challengers are thought of as relatively carefree individuals, but do care what people think, to an extent. The issue for them arises when people they love, admire, or respect try to change or shame them for their intense nature. Challengers, at their core, fear rejection just as much as the rest of us. And when you make them feel as if they don't belong because of things they can't change about themselves, it deeply hurts them. A Challenger once told me that one of the worst feelings he'd experienced was when others alluded to being embarrassed by his personality in the presence of others. Sometimes Challengers want to tease and cause a scene intentionally, but most of the time, they desire to just hang out like the rest of us. If you're close with a Challenger, whether they're your family, partner, or close friend, try not to unfairly judge them for their intensity. Even at their healthiest and most self-aware, Challengers will always be fiercely passionate, and they deserve to be loved for that. Embracing their intensity—and maybe even joining in on it every once in a while—will mean the world to them.

Always Be Genuine with Them

If you've ever tried to force a Challenger to feel an emotion they did not want to feel in the moment, I imagine that things did not end well for you. Type 8s need to feel safe, accepted, and free before being vulnerable with others, even if it's their dearest friend. When you see an emotion or area of a Challenger's life that needs to be addressed, one of the worst things you can do is demand an emotional response from them. Challengers don't like to be commanded, and commanding them can create deeply rooted mistrust and misunderstanding between you and them. Challengers desire to feel respected by those they care about in life, and one of the best ways you can show them respect is to simply be honest with them. As I mentioned earlier, many of us hold the preconceived notion that Challengers like it when people are upset with them or when they're verbally sparring with someone else. But Challengers are so unapologetically honest that sometimes they genuinely don't realize when they've said or done something to cause someone hurt. All of the Type 8s in my life would be absolutely crushed if they found out they'd insulted or disrespected someone and didn't initially realize it. Challengers make us aware of when they feel confused or hurt, and they expect the same level of authenticity from us. They're unafraid to approach you, so be unafraid to approach them. They will feel so valued and loved when you give them your genuine and honest emotions and thoughts.

THE PEACEMAKER

REASSURING, ACCEPTING,
AMENABLE, STABLE, DIPLOMATIC

CORE DESIRES:

To be unaffected, at peace, and connected

CORE FEARS:

Being cut off from love, being separated
from someone or something

ULTIMATE MOTIVATIONS:

To resist potential conflict, to sustain a
comfortable and balanced environment, to avoid
what may upset or disturb inner harmony

AFFIRMATION:

"My presence matters."

Our sweet Enneagram Type 9 friends are usually the ones that unintentionally blend into the background. Like true wallflowers, they show up in this world gently yet stubbornly. They usually struggle the most to determine their Enneagram type because they have a hard time recognizing their own personality traits and characteristics, since they often take on the attributes of the people and environment around them. Also known as "Peacemakers," Type 9s are the ones who listen, understand, and accept you no matter what. Incredibly agreeable, they avoid sharing their own personal opinions and preferences when they sense it could lead to tension with others. Type 9s take an optimistic and easygoing approach to life, and having a Peacemaker in your inner circle enriches and deepens your life in ways you could never have anticipated!

You Might Be a Peacemaker If . . .

- You wish you had a little bit more ambition in life. You tend to be happy with where you are, even if you know it may not be the best place for you.

- You have an incredibly goofy and sarcastic sense of humor that often surprises people.

- You tend to be busy—you're always going and doing and moving, but you struggle to get the most important things done every day because they can seem overwhelming.

- You have been told multiple times in life that you are incredibly stubborn, and you have no problem admitting it.

- You have very strong opinions and preferences, but

you don't usually share them, in an effort to avoid creating conflict.

- Someone asking you to choose where you would like to eat is one of your least favorite things in life.
- You are naturally drawn to ideas and beliefs that will help you maintain a sense of groundedness and inner peace.
- You hate to admit it, but you usually choose the path of least resistance.
- It's hard for you to see the value you bring to a group, because you often feel overshadowed by bolder personalities.
- You have a handful of artists, sports, or styles that you're completely dedicated to.
- Similar to Type 5s, you genuinely lose energy very quickly and have a hard time explaining to others why that is.
- You crave responsibility and growth, but you don't want the pressure and demands that come with it.

9W8 Although they still carry the same peaceful nature of a Type 9, they are driven more instinctually. They don't have as hard a time setting boundaries and taking risks, and they don't mind getting into a debate with you if the topic is something they are truly passionate about. Self-sacrificing, resourceful, and always cheering for the underdog, 9s who lean into their 8 wing are unstoppable!

9W1

9s who lean into their 1 wing have an intense conflict within themselves that they have a hard time voicing. They are more prone to perfectionism—maintaining peace means maintaining order—and they are very self-critical. Although they see both sides to everything, they usually have a set of morals to which they are dedicated. They may not share their personal opinions often, but they will never betray them. Type 9s who lean into their 1 wing are passionate about efficiency and their causes. Simply put, you want a 9W1 in your corner to share their quietly remarkable insights!

WHY PEACEMAKERS NEED SELF-CARE

Much like their Challenger friends, Peacemakers are prone to pushing themselves beyond their limits because they are not aware of what they truly want in life. This can cause them to end up in situations where they may be taken advantage of, or say "yes" to someone in order to avoid a possible argument or disagreement. "Going along to get along" can lead our Peacemakers down a path of self-numbing. Type 9s even tend to use self-care as a way to self-isolate and suppress what is truly bothering them. When Peacemakers instead utilize self-care as a tool for growth, they become awakened and passionate people. Connecting with their anger, sadness, joy, and enthusiasm—even if it seems like it would be overwhelming—will help Peacemakers discover their voice and true desires. Type 9s make great diplomats, presidents, and leaders, and it all starts by believing that their voice and presence matters in this world.

SELF-CARE PRACTICES FOR TYPE 9S

Find Your Balance

I would say the majority of Peacemakers struggle to find balance in their life, which is ironic, because that is what they crave most. Types 9s are always on the hunt for equanimity, tranquility, and peacefulness. They don't want one area of their life to feel heavier or more complicated; they want everything to be at the same level of emotion all of the time. This quest can confuse Peacemakers, because most of them probably feel like their life is anything but balanced. Many of them may even frequently find themselves in imbalanced lifestyles and situations. This is because as much as Peacemakers want balance in their life, they find comfort in what they already know. And usually in order to begin working toward balance, you have to actively work toward taking more risks. I think it's important to understand that, as a Peacemaker, if you want to make a change in your life, you have to choose to evolve! Balance won't just eventually find you, and it won't simply fall into place. Finding balance takes guts, and it can be a fight. It requires a change of pace, a change of mindset, and an acceptance of the uncertain. But it's worth fighting for so that you can continue to grow into your best and healthiest self.

Do a Brain Dump

Although they have a calm and collected exterior, Peacemakers usually have a lot on their mind at any given time. They're reminiscing, worrying, stressing, dreaming . . . they have thoughts and feelings they don't know how to express fully because they're also somewhat detached from their reality. One of the best things Type 9s can do for their mental health is what I sometimes refer to as "brain dump." To do a brain dump, grab a piece of paper (or a notebook or journal), sit, and write out everything that is inside your brain onto the pages. Don't worry about your words looking or sounding perfect. Don't worry about them being profound or "important" enough. Just connect to your inner dialogue, and write it all down. Brain dumps will not only help you create space to process but also space to create. After you're done, you can read all that you've been thinking about, and doing so may make those emotions that were once consuming you or tasks you were once worrying about feel less daunting. When you see these things written down, they become a little bit smaller. A little bit more manageable. This is important for Peacemakers to do, as they are easily overwhelmed by their responsibilities and feelings. Remember that you're still human. You're still creative. You're still capable. Put it all on the page first, and you'll feel more prepared and assured to go through all of it.

Have "Do Not Disturb" Time

Whether they are extroverted or introverted, Peacemakers highly value their alone time. They love spending time in a relaxing environment, uninterrupted by the pressures of life and relationships. The issue is, although having this time for themselves is what they ultimately crave, they don't know how to ask others to give it to them. In a way, Peacemakers can feel like their time, thoughts, and feelings are not their own. Rather, they belong to the people they love the most. When in an unhealthy state, they have a tendency to allow others to determine their feelings, thoughts, and use of their time, and they become disconnected from what they truly want in life. When they begin to believe that they do not "own" themselves in a sense, this can cause Peacemakers to become distant in relationships, even if they're seemingly present in them. Type 9s are often scared to admit to others when they need their space, because they don't want people to be offended by their request. In a way, Peacemakers also struggle with the fear of missing out, but they're really more fixated on the fear of being disconnected from the people they love. Finding the time to take care of their well-being means they risk disappointing someone, which would make a Peacemaker feel horrible. Peacemakers, you need to understand that your loved ones and true friends will value your alone time as much as you do, because they know it's good for you. While practicing this advice may be risking some current connections in your life, it will help you purge the relationships that are harmful to your well-being. I want to challenge all Peacemakers to find one night per week and dedicate it to self-care—whether self-care for you involves playing an instrument, taking a bubble bath, cleaning up your room, praying, or something entirely different. Call that block of time your "do not disturb" time, and don't let any external pressures prevent you from taking it. Trust me: you will be more present and feel more alive when you do so.

Savor Times of Coziness

Peacemakers are the most cozy of the Enneagram types, in my opinion. That may be hard to understand, but if you've ever met a Peacemaker, then you know they have a love for all the things that make life warm and snug.

This is actually a strength of Peacemakers—a soft strength, if you will—but it's also something they don't always know how to enjoy fully. They are aware of when a moment feels intimate and special, but they are often far from truly savoring the moment and experiencing all of the emotions it inspires at once. Peacemakers don't like to show or be affected by strong emotions, because these emotions feel so much more extreme to them than they do to other types. This is why it's important for Peacemakers, as they play cozy games and songs or as they read and watch cozy things, to take a moment and ask themselves if they're seeking enjoyment from the coziness, or if they're using coziness as a way to numb how they're really feeling inside. The comforts of life are meant to provide a sense of safety to what feels uncertain, but this can never replace the security that comes from connecting with your authentic self. So, Peacemakers, learn to truly be present in the moments of coziness you create. Allow yourself to feel things because of your environment. Let the inner peace you are attempting to preserve be affected by the emotions and realities of life. True peace will come only when you allow and accept whatever is going on within you to rise to the surface.

Develop a New Habit or Daily Routine

Peacemakers have a hard time with creating new and lasting habits. Whether they are striving to eat healthier, exercise more, or add new rhythms to their life, committing to a regular practice when they struggle to maintain high energy levels in general is difficult for them. With that, they are also incredibly stubborn and don't like to feel that something or someone is telling them how to live their life. In reality, though, Peacemakers are quick to give up on themselves in these situations, not because they don't believe they can succeed, but because the new situations are uncomfortable for them. They have learned to thrive in familiarity, and changes that bring up negative self-talk they're not familiar with will cause them to retreat to an old habit or routine that *may* feel more comfortable but is not necessarily benefiting their mental well-being. That's why I'm calling on all Peacemakers to commit not just to a cleanse or diet or thirty-day challenge but to a lifestyle shift. Make that positive change you've been putting off. Make it, and don't turn back. Peacemakers underestimate their ability to do things like this, but all it takes is some momentum to get a Type 9 going. Once they're sold on something, they're sold for life. So leave the habits you know aren't improving your life behind you, and instead finally commit to the new habits you believe will keep you sane, safe, and healthy. Become sold on your self-care—because you deserve it.

Be Unstoppable

Peacemakers, contrary to popular belief, don't in fact have a hard time being firm or assertive. They have an extremely strong belief system about the world, and, with good mental health, they are unafraid to speak about their beliefs with others. This is because, though it is their personal belief, they are relatively detached from the situation. But the second their character, their relationship, or their passion comes into question, they have a tendency to sit and be silent so they can keep their thoughts and feelings safe. Developing their own agenda to fight for what they believe in, especially when faced with potential questioning from those they care about, is difficult for them. The truth is, though, once Peacemakers can get themselves going, they are unstoppable in their pursuits. One of my Peacemaker friends single-handedly organized a public fundraising event in the wake of Hurricane Harvey's devastation of our community—not because it was her job or someone asked her to do it. She had her own idea, and once she got started on it, she didn't stop working on it until it was finished. And guess what? The event was *awesome*! She brought together more than ten vendors, five different live musicians, and raised more than $4,000 for victims of the hurricane. I saw her work harder than I ever had during that time, and it was amazing to witness because it wasn't for anyone else's agenda but her own. Once she put her mind to it, she couldn't be stopped, and she ended up helping so many people. I hope her story will help you realize you can and should do the same.

Voice Your Preferences

Peacemakers usually don't act like they care about things such as what restaurant their friends want to eat at or what time they should all meet up, but most Peacemakers, when honest with themselves, actually have strong preferences when faced with these kinds of decisions. They maintain a particular "aesthetic," if you will, and they ideally would rather not stray from that aesthetic. Whether it's the way they dress or the things that they eat, they like their way of being and don't have a desire to change it. But Peacemakers want to be perceived as nonchalant and flexible, so these preferences will fall to the wayside when they're around people who have asserted their preferences already. A small self-care challenge I have for Peacemakers is: The next time you're with a group of people and a decision needs to be made, before you say, "I don't care" or "I'm fine with anything," ask yourself, "Do I care? Am I fine with anything?" Sometimes the answer genuinely is, "I really don't care right now, and I would be fine with anything." Other times, you *do* want something in particular deep down, but feel too selfish to share it. Learn to know those differences, and let others in on them. Learn to know why it is you don't feel like those preferences are important, even though they are.

Determine Your Worth

All Enneagram types struggle to share their voice or believe in themselves from time to time, but this is a lifelong battle for Peacemakers. Peacemakers innately believe their voice isn't worth lending to conversations and that their actions won't make a real impact in the world. They believe this because growing up they usually were the most soft-spoken person in the room, and they often went unnoticed or unconsidered. Peacemakers have a tendency to think that, because of their past experiences, other people determine whether or not they are important. In other words, it takes someone else recognizing Peacemakers' talents or skills to validate that they're worthy, rather than believing they are worthy themselves. I think we've all believed this about ourselves to a certain degree. But the truth is, the people you want to deem you worthy may never deem you worthy—not because you aren't valuable, but because people are human. A girl I went to camp with in high school struggled with this idea a lot. She confessed that she felt as though she was meant to be mediocre, and she'd just learned to accept that. When our camp counselor heard her say this, she looked her in the eyes with firmness and respect, and said, "The second you start believing you are mediocre is when you become mediocre." So, to all of the sweet Peacemakers reading this, I want you to remember that as much as we crave approval from others or believe we have nothing special to offer, *we* are the ones who determine that our voice is valuable and actions are meaningful. We determine our worth.

Open Up to Your Friends

Type 9s are actually very active within their friend groups and inner circles. They love hanging out with their close friends, and could even do so for hours on end. Similar to Type 8s, though, Peacemakers have a hard time participating in mutually vulnerable conversations. A Peacemaker may be a part of your friend group for years, but when you really think about how well you know them or how they're doing, you might find yourself realizing you don't actually know much about them at all. Type 9s are uncomfortable sharing their personal life with others, even with those closest to them, because they don't find it necessary. They figure you're interested in other things, and they would never want to bore you or burden you with their feelings or problems. But, Peacemakers, your pain, your story, your quirks—all of it—matters. Your friends love you not just because you are there for them but because you're you! True friends genuinely care about you and want to know who you are on the inside. They want to know the heavy and the light. So take some time to analyze whether you're actually present in your friendships. Do you only hang out, laugh, and have fun? Or do you discuss, confide, reach out, and dig deep as well?

Know When to Walk Away

This tip may sound kind of harsh, but believe me when I tell you I have never met a Peacemaker who has not needed to leave a job because they were struggling or being taken advantage of while at work. As you know, Peacemakers can be quick to settle into comfortable routines, and then stay in them longer than they should, so moving on from something like a job can be a very strenuous decision for them. It can take them years to finally step away from something that was harmful to begin with. So, Peacemakers who are reading this, take some time to do a little life audit. Are you happy? Are you satisfied? Is your job overall truly mentally and physically healthy for you? If your job is not of concern, then take stock of the friendships, relationships, and organizations you're involved in . . . are they healthy? Are they beneficial? Are they enhancing your life or making it miserable? Be honest with yourself. My husband is a Peacemaker, and he has gone through seasons of this struggle multiple times. Know that as you get older, recognizing when it's time to walk away doesn't get easier, and neither does the actual walking away, but you will become stronger for it. So if you feel like you need permission from somebody out there, here it is. Quit that job. Leave that relationship. Move on from the past. Cut out that toxic friend from your life. I can promise you'll always grow from doing so, and you'll grow beautifully.

Remember That Your Presence Matters

Out of all of the types, I think Peacemakers walk through one of the most heartbreaking core fears one can have: believing and assuming that their presence does not matter to others. Whether they were told this verbally, communicated this nonverbally, or experienced a series of events that fostered this belief, Type 9s struggle to remember that they do matter. Life is loud and busy. People can be ambitious and cutthroat. Peacemakers can feel as though they are swirling in the sea of everyone else's agendas, which causes them to detach from their own sense of self. This detachment in turn gives Peacemakers the idea that they don't really matter to anyone or anything—that they're always the "extra" or the "supporting role," never the main character, never in the spotlight. If there is anything I want Peacemakers to take away from this book, it is that your presence in the world always matters. When you show up, it makes a difference in the world. When you smile, it brightens a room. When you laugh, it captivates us. Remember: you don't have to earn or qualify for worthiness; you matter simply because you exist and make all our lives better.

HOW TO TAKE CARE OF
THE TYPE 9 IN YOUR LIFE

Be Respectful of Their
Struggles with Conflict

If you have a Type 9 in your life, you know they don't like to make waves in their relationships or in life in general. Although they desire to be affirmed or recognized by others, they are constantly thinking of ways they can avoid potentially rocking the boat or making people upset with what they do or say. Peacemakers also have a hard time being honest about their emotions and thoughts, and they struggle to take ownership of their actions. This is because they are genuinely afraid that their actions or expressed feelings will jeopardize the connection they have with those they love. In fact, I believe their drive to always keep the peace and not ruffle feathers comes from a place of such strong longing for connection, and fear that they will lose it, that they pretend they are fine as long as everyone else seems to be happy. All of this is to say that although Peacemakers tend to avoid conflict, they are not apathetic people. As Peacemakers grow, it'll become easier for them to use their voice, not be afraid of their mistakes, and express their feelings. In the meantime, remember that Peacemakers are avoidant of conflict because of how deeply it affects and depletes them. No other number within the Enneagram becomes more drained and exhausted from the anxiety conflict causes than a Peacemaker. So give them the time they need to process conflict when they're going through it. Give them the space to recover after it's over. Engage them with patience, just as they would do for you. Not making them feel guilty for how conflict affects them will mean a lot to them. It will show how much respect you have for them—how much you're willing to stay in this with them without judgment or criticism of how they handle things.

Ask Them Questions and Listen to Them

As with any personality or Enneagram type, feeling as though you are going unnoticed, unheard, and unrecognized is a horrible thing to experience. Peacemakers continually feel as though they don't matter because everyone else's needs and voices in a room can easily overtake theirs. People are always telling them to speak up, answer questions, be more involved, be more engaged, and share their thoughts, but when a Type 9 attempts to do so, they are usually interrupted by the same people who've been telling them to do these things. This is hurtful for a Peacemaker to experience, and only bolsters their tendency to believe that who they are is not actually valued or heard. So when you ask a Peacemaker in your life a question, let them think about it. Let them answer it without interruption. Let them tell their story in full. Listen to them. Remember the details. React to their answers. Think of follow-up questions. Show them that you're not only interested in what they have to say but that you hear them as well. Show them you believe what they are telling you is valuable, that they are valuable, that their voice and conversation matters to you. Avoid forcing Peacemakers to speak, and avoid speaking over them. Be intentional, and listen well.

Always Be Honest with Them

Peacemakers hate disappointing people. They only want you to be happy when you're with them. When faced with making a decision, to which they're naturally resistant, they want your support and attention, and they want your honesty—because if you aren't honest with them about what you want and then you express dissatisfaction with their decision, it will make them feel like their guts have been ripped out of them. Extreme, but true! So please don't be afraid to be honest with Peacemakers, and avoid behavioral patterns that keep them guessing about what you really want when they've already asked you. Nothing can upset or hurt a Peacemaker more than dishonesty and disingenuousness. Peacemakers want to know where they stand with you, and they want to know that you're happy in the midst of it. So for all of the precious Peacemakers in your life, show them that you will love them no matter what with your honesty. Even in disagreement, even in vulnerability, even in conflict, when you show up with authentic honesty, it shows them that you are there for them and rooting for them despite anything that happens or any decision they make. That you don't want conflict as much as they don't.

A NOTE FOR ALL TYPES

At the end of all of this, I want to say that I hope you know you are loved. I hope that because of one sentence or chapter in this book, your head rests a little easier tonight. I hope your creative or professional endeavor comes to fruition. I hope you send the audition tape. I hope you quit that toxic job and start your dream career. I hope you take the first step toward being more vulnerable with your friends. I hope you get to go on that solo trip. I hope you start to see how much value you have, apart from a personality test, apart from the behavioral patterns and cycles that come most naturally to you. I hope and pray you stand taller—that you finally break through the ceiling you've been hitting for so long, that you let others see how bright you are, that you finally let the buds turn into blossoms.

I hope this book helps you, even in the smallest of ways, to enjoy life a little more often, love others a little bit deeper, and find yourself worthy of self-care.

ACKNOWLEDGMENTS

This book is a community effort. It belongs to the thousands of wonderful people who have been supporting me for the past two years. I'm truly honored that you trusted me with your stories over and over again. I'm humbled by your continued generosity and kindness. I thank God for you every day.

I'm also particularly grateful for the wonderful team around me:

Thank you to Noah Wilcox, my husband. Every late night, every time I doubted myself, through everything. You are my person, my best friend. I literally could not have done this without you. I love you, Bean.

To my agents, Aemilia Philips and Mackenzie Brady Watson, for the countless moments of guidance, validation, and belief in this project and in me.

To the Simon & Schuster team and the Tiller Press imprint—Lauren Hummel, Theresa DiMasi, Sam Ford, Kate Davids, Marlena Brown, Laura Flavin, and Patrick Sullivan—for the support and opportunity.

To my incredible community online, my patrons, and those in the "Enneagram Friends" Facebook group, thank you for continuously fostering amazing conversations surrounding the Enneagram and for committing to being vulnerable and available to me and to one another. Without you, none of this would be possible.

To my parents, Keith and Lisa Smet, for praying for me and always believing in me. I am forever grateful to you. And to the countless friends and family who encouraged and supported me during this project.

To God: my life, this book, everything, is for Him, by Him, and through Him.